DO YOU
BELIEVE?

BY ROBERT NOLAND

Experience the full power of the cross

40-DAY DEVOTIONAL

D1158469

Do You Believe?
Experience the Full Power of the Cross

Based on the motion picture *Do You Believe?* by Pure Flix Entertainment. All content from the movie used by permission.

ISBN: 978-1-4245-4986-3 (paperback)
ISBN: 978-1-4245-5040-1 (e-book)

Published by BroadStreet Publishing Group, LLC
Racine, Wisconsin, USA
www.broadstreetpublishing.com

Cover design by Chris Garborg at www.garborgdesign.com
Interior typesetting by Katherine Lloyd at www.TheDESKonline.com

Stock or custom editions of BroadStreet Publishing titles may be purchased in bulk for educational, business, ministry, fundraising, or sales promotional use. For information, please e-mail info@broadstreetpublishing.com.

Printed in the United States of America.

15 16 17 18 19 20 7 6 5 4 3 2 1

Contents

M ark 1:35 tells us Jesus got up early in the morning and went away alone to pray. One of the most life-changing spiritual disciplines in which you can invest is a daily and dedicated time alone with God. No distractions. No devices or noise and no one else around. Here are a few steps for success in utilizing this book.

1: Decide to commit. Purpose to use this book for the next forty days—one day at a time. Set aside the time to make a habit of engaging with the words contained here. If you miss a day, just pick back up. Don't quit—commit.

2: Pick a time. While spending time with God first thing in the morning is best to set the pace for your day, choose a time that is optimum for your schedule. You may need to experiment a bit, but pick a time and stick with it.

3: Choose a place. You need a quiet and peaceful setting. Get away from distractions. Turn off the phone. The place is crucial for you to be focused and comfortable as you engage with God.

4: Read. Take in the content—every word. Carefully read the Bible verses. If you prefer to use your own version of Scripture each day, feel free to do so.

5: Journal. There is journal space included with every day. Answer the closing questions, then write out anything you hear from God or feel you need to express. Journaling is a powerful tool God can use to help you process your spiritual walk.

6: *Pray.* Allow time to speak with God and tell him everything as you would a best friend. If you have never spent time in personal prayer, the next forty days could revolutionize your spiritual growth.

7: *Listen and obey.* Close your time with a quiet moment to hear God speak. Then obey what you hear and "walk out" what he tells you each day. The goal is to complete these forty days and allow Jesus to change your life!

> Here's what I want you to do: Find a quiet, secluded place so you won't be tempted to role-play before God. Just be there as simply and honestly as you can manage. The focus will shift from you to God, and you will begin to sense his grace. —Matthew 6:6 MSG

SYMBOL
OF SALVATION

Matthew is a pastor, sitting at his desk at night. The house is very quiet. He is intent in his thoughts and appears burdened. The small desk lamp illuminates a legal pad. As we move closer, we see he has filled the page by drawing a simple outline of a cross. Underneath it, he has written a bold message: Do You Believe?

Humans have always used symbols to represent important elements of their existence. Few have stood the test of time and lasted throughout generations, becoming unmistakable, nonverbal icons to create a recognizable image of deep meaning.

One of the most enduring symbols of all time is the cross. But different people understand different meanings based on their life experience, so let's ask …

When you hear the word *cross*, do you tend to think about …

… a fashionable piece of jewelry?

… a classic element of church architecture?

… a representation of a religion long since left behind?

… the physical instrument God used for the spiritual redemption of your soul?

For you, is the cross's meaning …

… historical?

… religious?

… personal?

While your answer to the latter question could certainly be "all three," there is a likelihood one rings the *most* true for you.

As we begin this forty-day journey centered on the cross of Christ, evaluating how you feel, what you think, and how deep your belief goes is important to how impactful these days will be for you. One of the vital keys for experiencing life change will be the level of honesty and transparency you allow with God. He already sees you and knows you intimately, but opening your heart to him will make all the difference.

A distinguishing focal point of the cross is that it is not associated with any belief system other than Christianity and with no person other than Jesus Christ, the Son of God. Throughout church history, and in art of all forms, the cross is presented in two ways.

First is with Jesus hanging on its beams, representing his suffering, sacrifice, and eventual death. Second, and where we find many of our artistic images, is the empty cross. While this could seem to denote an absence of Christ, it is actually showing the opposite—a presence. Christ has risen! He is alive and seated at the right hand of God. The cross and the tomb are now empty so that our hearts can be full and our lives fulfilled.

Few will debate or argue the historical fact that Jesus hung on the cross and gave his life. The only disagreement for people is whether or not his death meant anything for mankind.

The simple, rough-hewn wooden beams strapped and nailed together convey a powerful and prevailing image of God's intervention in the world. While the cross may instigate different responses, the image has remained a respected, valued, and consistent reminder of man's problem met with God's presence. But the real question is not what does the cross mean throughout history for the world, but rather, what does the cross mean to *you*?

Regardless of your own personal perspective, this cruel device of torture and execution the authorities used to eliminate Jesus actually was the instrument God wielded to surgically remove the sting of sin and death forever from those who would choose to believe him.

Today, let us not think of the cross as a symbol, an image, or an icon, but rather, a personal choice each one of us must make. So our closing question today comes from the film's title and Pastor Matthew's drawing ... Do you believe?

Whether you feel you are hanging on to life by a thread and desperately searching for answers or you are a vibrant, mature follower of Christ simply looking to grow, we must continually ask ourselves what we believe and what the cross means to us—today. This day!

> And when he was living as a man, he humbled himself and was fully obedient to God, even when that caused his death—death on a cross. —Philippians 2:8 NCV

⊹

With as honest of an answer as you can give, complete the sentence below on your journal page, while expressing any other thoughts you have on today's reading.

For me, the cross of Christ means ...

FROM BAGGAGE TO BELIEF

S everal of the characters in *Do You Believe?* struggle with the concepts of God, faith, and belief. Regrets, tragedy, betrayal, disappointment, and personal pain give people the opportunity to choose to become disillusioned, cynical, and doubt ridden. We quickly see spiritual "baggage" has most definitely been created at some point and negatively challenges any encounter with belief. Our culture, both inside and outside of the church, is filled with people who fit this description. The systemic problem this creates in society is best said in the old adage, "Hurt people hurt people."

The character, Maggie, a young lady who is pregnant, struggles to understand why Matthew, the pastor, is trying to help her. She tells him, "You are a freak." "What do you mean?" he asks. "Nobody helps people just to help them," Maggie firmly states. "Yeah, well," he explains, "I'm a Christian." "So are most of the people who ignore me," she snaps back.

On one occasion, Jesus was traveling alone and went through Samaria. He found a well and sat down to rest. A Samaritan woman came to draw water. As Jesus began to speak with her, she proved she knew the Law well and also the deep lines drawn between Jews and Samaritans. As the conversation went on, Jesus encountered this woman's spiritual and personal baggage, until finally ...

> The woman said, "Well, at least I know that the Messiah will come—the one they call Christ—and when he does, he will explain everything to us." Then Jesus told her, "I am the Messiah!" —John 4:25–26 TLB

One of the toughest aspects of constant disbelief is to know when you have finally encountered the truth for the opportunity to believe! Maggie and the Samaritan woman were being brought to the place of seeing the reality of God for the very first time. After years of being ignored by people, even religious ones, God was showing he never ignores anyone!

In your own personal journey, have you had a hurtful or negative situation with a church, a minister, or someone who has called himself or herself a Christian? Was there someone in your life who you feel tried to force you into a belief? Or maybe you felt "guilted" into a decision? Was your family spiritually "neutral" and never gave you much opportunity to believe in anything? Maybe you were raised to have a strong, authentic faith in Christ?

Regardless of your answer, for each of us at some point, we must make the choice to have our own faith—a personal belief that we own—or even decide to reject any faith we once had. The decision cannot be made by our grandmother, dad, pastor, or priest. Those people may influence us, but they can't ultimately be responsible for our decision as to whether or not to believe.

In this moment, as you read and consider today's thoughts

and questions for your own heart, no one is pressuring you; no one is telling you what to do; no one is placing an expectation on your answer. God has given you the freedom to choose. He won't force you; he won't demand a certain answer; he won't make you believe in him. With Maggie, the pastor was giving her the *opportunity* to see what Christian love and grace can truly be like. Just as with the Samaritan woman when Jesus gave her the *opportunity* to believe.

> Then the woman left her waterpot beside the well and went back to the village and told everyone, "Come and meet a man who told me everything I ever did! Can this be the Messiah?" —John 4:28–29 TLB

For this woman, belief was coming.

The great news the cross of Christ offers is God loves you. So Jesus died for you.

He has shown his belief in you; the question remains—do you believe in him?

There is another old saying that goes, "Life will make you better or bitter." Who gets to make the choice for you? You do.

Complete the sentence below on your journal page, along with any other thoughts you have on your own belief.

Today, in owning my own faith, I believe ...

IMPRINT
OR FINGERPRINT

Some might view faith as simply an imprint on our lives—a broad belief of some kind, determining a person's value system. But for the follower of Christ, faith is like a fingerprint—a unique, customized, one-of-a-kind testimony God has fashioned.

At an art gallery, the guests are looking at painting after painting, so the art might appear from a distance to be similar. Yet upon close inspection, each piece is uniquely different. This is a picture of what faith in God creates in us as well. Those who call themselves Christians can look just like anyone else, but once you hear the distinct experience of the soul that God brings about, a masterpiece is unveiled. A once-blank canvas is now brought to a personal portrait of vivid and vibrant life.

Today, there is a question you must settle for yourself: Is *your* faith an imprint or a fingerprint? Do you have a testimony of God's unique work for your personal salvation? Is Jesus a major character in your life's plot?

Malachi, the street preacher who carries the cross, tells Matthew, the pastor, "True believin' ain't just knowin' about it or preachin' about it. No. True believin' means accepting that

Christ carried this cross, was nailed to this cross, died on this cross … for you!"

There is a God-shaped void inside each of us, created by our inherent disobedience to God—what we call "sin." No one taught us to lie, manipulate, or demand our own way. We just know naturally how to behave that way. All of us try to fill this void through many methods—with a talent, skill, relationship, or by pretending to be someone we're not. We can try to fill it with drugs, alcohol, materialism, illicit sex, or other damaging habits. The dilemma is none of these give us real, lasting peace; they just create more problems and pain.

> For all have sinned and fall short of the glory of God.
> —Romans 3:23 NIV

To add insult to injury, we cannot see on our own that God is the answer to this emptiness. So his Spirit draws and leads us to realize our need for him.

With that knowledge, then what is the answer?

Thomas said to him, "Lord, how can we know the way?" Jesus answered, "I am the way and the truth and the life. No one comes to the Father except through me" (John 14:5–6 NIV). Jesus states in quite clear terms that he is the only gateway to God.

Romans 6:23 tells us the price paid for sin is death, which ultimately means eternal separation from God. Because God is holy, he requires punishment by death for the choices we have made. So as the answer, Jesus came to give himself as the final sacrifice for us (Hebrews 7:27). Jesus died so you wouldn't have to. Christ died in your place (Romans 5:8).

Christ arrives right on time to make this happen. He didn't, and doesn't, wait for us to get ready. He presented himself for this sacrificial death when we were far too weak and rebellious to do anything to get ourselves ready. —Romans 5:6 MSG

Receiving Jesus Christ as your Lord and Savior is the best choice you will ever make. But turning your life over to him is just the beginning. He wants a relationship with you. If you're ready to find your faith fingerprint, you can pray this prayer:

Dear God, I know I have disobeyed you and need your forgiveness. I choose to turn from my sin and receive today the gift of salvation and eternal life you are offering me. Thank you for dying for me, saving me, and changing my life. In Jesus' name, amen.

If you prayed that prayer, you have done what Malachi would call "true believin'." Now, go tell someone. Call a pastor, a Christian friend, or a family member. Let someone know.

If after reading today you are confident you are already a Christ-follower, consider sharing the gospel with someone you know who needs to hear it.

In your journal, write down the date of your salvation (as best you recall) and then continue writing your thoughts to this open-ended sentence:

I know God has created my faith fingerprint because …

A MATTER OF LIFE AND DEATH

Would you agree the following statement is true? "The vast majority of people are afraid to die."

Maybe the word *afraid* is too mild? *Terrified* might be a more fitting description. Yes, even those who profess faith and claim to know exactly where they are going in eternity may dread death. Although we will all face this great unknown, it remains the nemesis of man.

Yet the more prevailing and provoking question we face on a daily basis is actually, "Are we afraid to truly live?" In our chaotic culture, so many look as if they begrudge their very existence, merely getting by and surviving only to go through it all again the next day, and the next day, and the next.

Gang member Kriminal holds a pistol to Malachi's forehead. But Malachi never flinches or blinks. His response to the young man is not one of fear, panic, or cowering, but rather he simply and confidently states, "I'm ready. Are you?" Rather than Kriminal unnerving Malachi, the opposite occurs. The tables turn. How can someone seemingly have no fear, not even cringe, while staring death in the face?

The apostle Paul wrote his letter to the church at Philippi while he was in prison. He was arrested due to the hostility of the government and the religious system toward the gospel. As they had been with Jesus, the authorities continued to be threatened by the message and power displayed by Christ's followers.

While modern scholars debate the location of where Paul was held prisoner, he was, nonetheless, incarcerated and awaiting a trial that could result in a conviction and execution. Paul knew that, literally at any time, he could go on trial and be swiftly sentenced to death. From such a place, he wrote:

> And I trust that my life will bring honor to Christ, whether I live or die. For to me, living means living for Christ, and dying is even better. But if I live, I can do more fruitful work for Christ. So I really don't know which is better. I'm torn between two desires: I long to go and be with Christ, which would be far better for me. But for your sakes, it is better that I continue to live. —Philippians 1:20–24 NLT

The apostle Paul is debating with himself over whether living or dying is more beneficial for him! He finally comes down to the simple conclusion that staying to get more work done for God's glory would be best. But while at face value this "conversation with himself" might sound a bit arrogant to an immature ear, it actually reveals what a deep and intimate love Paul had for Jesus. The spirit of Paul's words was simply: "I want to leave here to be with you, Lord, forever. Yet I will stay and live for you if that is what you want; even here in prison, awaiting a possible death sentence."

We must always remember when reading Scripture that,

as is clearly seen in this passage by Paul, we are being taught how to think, how to behave, and how to live as mature believers. Paul was passing both attitude and action toward life and death on to his beloved younger brothers and sisters in the faith. His suffering was producing sanctification in the church. Amazingly, centuries later, we have the privilege of gaining the benefit of his wisdom as well.

The great lesson here for all believers is that this exact mind-set, or maybe more accurately, "heart-set," is completely available to each of us. You are invited to come to the place of maturity where you agree with Paul and declare, "For to me, living is living for Christ, and dying is even better." God's love and grace can lead us to the confident and secure place where Malachi found himself—looking a gunman in the eye and announcing, "I'm ready. Are you?"

In your journal, complete this sentence and write out your thoughts on life and death.

For me today, living for Christ means …

RECEPTION TO REVELATION

We see a slow pan of the Chicago skyline at night—the "Magnificent Mile" along Lake Michigan's waterfront. Millions of lights are twinkling against the darkness, coupled with thousands of cars in traffic and people walking, hurriedly going about their lives. We hear Pastor Matthew speak, "I often wonder why it is we're drawn to things. Take this city, for example. There are ten million people here, ten million souls, each of them searching for some sort of meaning in their lives. But how many actually find it?"

The term *belief* or *believe* gets a bit tricky, doesn't it? The word has taken on so many levels of connotation that it feels quite watered down. In fact, the word *believe* today is better interpreted by judging the words *around it* in a sentence, rather than *the word* itself. For example, we might say, "I believe I mailed the check last Tuesday," or "I believe the doctor may be right," or "I believe when I die, I'm going to heaven." Broad range in the depth of the meaning, wouldn't you agree?

Let's define a term—*belief system*. A belief system is a mental and spiritual state of mind from which you derive some or all of your rules and principles for living. This could be a philosophy or a religion. Typically it involves some kind of god, but may just be a manner of how one thinks and approaches life. In fact, atheism—the belief that there is no god—and agnosticism—someone who is neutral to the concept of a god—are belief systems.

All past, present, and future belief systems have one pattern in common: as a nonbeliever you are ignorant of the necessary knowledge needed to be enlightened. So you must hear and receive the information, which is then either rejected or received.

Reception of the information can become revelation—the full acceptance of the belief system as personal truth. Reception ends the ignorance. Revelation begins the belief. Most belief systems end here. Once you have received and accepted the information and are enlightened, you are officially in the club!

Let's recap the info so far …

For any belief system, you choose rejection or reception.
Reception can bring revelation.
Revelation brings belief.
Belief can bring a greater level of reception. And so it goes.

But Jesus came along and added another step, a new step. Consider this: How do you know if something is true in your life or in someone else's? Can you see belief? Of course not. But you can see obedience to the belief—the action following the motivation. You can see the knowledge carried out into action. James expressed the concept of ignorance to application perfectly:

> But don't just listen to God's word. You must do what
> it says. Otherwise, you are only fooling yourselves.
> —James 1:22 NLT

Christianity established itself as a belief system that required another step past knowledge—actual obedience. This step of action demands much more of our lives. We must think differently than simply being a religious person who must follow rules.

Here's a great example of Christ offering the command and explaining the application:

> Let me give you a new command: Love one another. In the same way I loved you, you love one another. This is how everyone will recognize that you are my disciples—when they see the love you have for each other. —John 13:34–35 MSG

Pastor Matthew talked about the few who truly find the meaning of life. The daily actions we take in Jesus' name prove his life is indeed alive in us.

Below is a list of basic Christian beliefs. Take a moment to evaluate your own level of application. Where and how do you need to grow? In your journal today, write out a prayer or a goal for each area of how you can move your beliefs toward action.

Prayer
Bible reading
Worship
Giving
Ministry

BLOOD-RED RANSOM

P astor Matthew stands before his congregation with a fire in his eyes, ignited by a renewed passion and fervor for his faith. Behind him stands a large wooden cross. He says, "The cross is a gift. The greatest gift of all. It's forgiveness, redemption, new life. And it was paid for with blood."

Throughout Scripture, we read continual accounts of animal sacrifices, placed on the altar and killed as a substitution for the death of the sinner. For sins to be forgiven by God, blood has to be shed (Hebrews 9:22). Something has to die for the disobedience. God, in his mercy, allowed an animal's blood to be accepted as the atonement.

Can you imagine in our beautiful, elaborate, stain-glassed sanctuaries today, having a blood-red and rancid altar where animals' lifeblood was spilled out for our sins? A megachurch would be sacrificing at the altar for days!

God decided his only Son, Jesus Christ, would be the final sacrifice offered for sin. We don't kill animals anymore on our altars, because the Lamb of God offered his life to end the bloodshed—once and for all.

Pastor Matthew continues, "Yet, when most of us look at the cross, we want the blood gone. We're ashamed of it. The blood that my sins—and yours—required as the price of our ransom."

We've all seen the countless movies where the plot centers on a wealthy and powerful person's family member being kidnapped. The villain's goal is to trade the life of the victim for something of great value to the family—a ransom. The kidnapped one becomes leverage for the villain. We've also seen many times where the hero is working feverishly against the clock to locate the kidnapper before the price is paid.

Imagine the moment when Jesus died, his blood shed, and his body broken. The enemy of God, the villain of man—Satan—believes he has won. God's plan appears to have failed, and now all mankind is forever doomed to hell.

For three days, Satan was allowed to believe that his plot, carried out through Judas, had worked. But … on that third morning … the ground shook … the stone rolled back … the giant curtain that separated God from man in the Holy of Holies was ripped—from the top to the bottom. The hero was alive! He had personally paid the ransom for us all. Satan was ultimately vanquished and his fate was forever sealed. Death defeated.

Matthew was right. We are ashamed of the sin that required Christ's blood be shed, which then taints how we view the cross. That's why we attempt to hide our dirty deeds, murderous thoughts, and self-centered intentions. It's why we say we're "doing fine" when we may be dying inside. Yet, ironically, that same blood Christ shed provides for us to never be ashamed again! We are free and forgiven. No more bloodshed. The ransom for our souls is paid!

There is therefore now no condemnation to those who are in Christ Jesus. —Romans 8:1 NKJV

Do you "beat yourself up" over your sins? Do you live guilt-ridden over the past or any present-day behavior? Is there an addiction clouding your heart?

If God is willing to exonerate you of everything you have ever done, are doing, and will do in the future, what is stopping you from letting go and forgiving yourself? Today can be the day you truly receive all God has to offer and escape the guilt and shame. The cell door has been unlocked; you just need to get up and walk out, never to return again. There will never be a better time to be set free than right now!

And they sang in a mighty chorus: "Worthy is the Lamb who was slaughtered—to receive power and riches and wisdom and strength and honor and glory and blessing." —Revelation 5:12 NLT

In your journal, complete these sentences and write out any feelings regarding past and present sin, guilt, and shame.
Lord Jesus, please forgive me for …
I give you these burdens now …

BAND-AIDS ON
BULLET WOUNDS

I n the emergency room, Dr. Thomas Farell enters with the air and attitude of a symphony conductor. Sarcastic with a hint of arrogance, he quips, "Eating Chinese takeout with a severe food allergy. I'd like to try 'suicidal' for $200, Alex." Elena, the nurse, reports, "EMTs already pushed five milligrams of epinephrine." The doctor responds, "Anybody bother to tell them that's a lot of adrenaline for a girl this size?" Another nurse answers, "They had trouble maintaining her airway." "That's why it's called anaphylaxis," Farell continues. "My guess is she couldn't care less whether we save her." Elena, surprised at his calloused view, asks, "How can you make an assumption like that?" The doctor stops and points to a grouping of scars on Lacey's wrists, showing from beneath her bracelets. Turning his gaze back to Elena, he condescendingly snaps, "Do you have a better theory you'd like to share, nurse?" Elena, now intimidated, just shakes her head and continues to work.

We could look at anyone's physical scars—the number of them and their placement—and make assumptions. Sometimes we'd be right and sometimes wrong. While it is difficult to get through life with no physical scars of any sort, all of us end up with a different type of scar—the ones on our hearts.

These scars can be created by cuts from …

An abusive parent

A jealous sibling

A bitter teacher

An insecure friend

A wayward family member

A cyber bully

Trying to heal our personal scars can often feel like putting a Band-Aid on a bullet wound. It only works for so long.

Regardless of where they came from, you know your scars well. You know who cut you, the circumstances, and possibly even the day and time. Maybe for you, someone continued the pattern of abuse over years. Whether you have a few nicks or severe lacerations, scars can become infected, define us, limit our relationships, and even create distrust of God.

When you see a physical scar, you know the cut has healed, but there's a deformity left on the skin. The problem with scars of the heart is you see them only in and through a person's behavior. A physical scar may look bad, but it no longer causes pain. A scar on the heart can cause pain every day.

Jesus Christ understands scars. As God, he could have avoided them altogether. But he didn't. He also understands what it takes to heal even the most painful of scars.

Isaiah prophesied about Christ, offering a surprising picture of what the Messiah would be like and what would be done to him:

There was nothing attractive about him, nothing to cause us to take a second look. He was looked down on and passed over, a man who suffered, who knew

pain firsthand. One look at him and people turned away. We looked down on him, thought he was scum. But the fact is, it was *our* pains he carried—*our* disfigurements, all the things wrong with *us*. We thought he brought it on himself, that God was punishing him for his own failures. But it was our sins that did that to him, that ripped and tore and crushed him—*our sins*! He took the punishment, and that made us whole. Through his bruises we get healed.
—Isaiah 53:2–5 MSG

Don't miss the words and phrases here—not attractive, no second look, looked down on, passed over, suffering, pain, ripped, tore, crushed, bruises. But while the picture painted is horrible, don't miss the ending—he took our sins, made us whole, and we are healed.

Life is going to create scars—external and internal. It's what we do with the scars that makes the difference. It's how we respond to the scars that can change our lives; allowing God to do what only he can do—heal us. God doesn't make us forget painful memories, but he can heal us from feeling the pain every day.

⊕

In your journal section, write down your deepest "heart scars" that cause you pain.

Have you given those to the Lord? Have you stopped hiding them and instead offered him your pain? Who might need to see your scars so you can tell that person about Jesus' healing?

Next, write out a prayer for what you need God to do with your scars and your pain.

HANGING
IN THE BALANCE

Bobby is a paramedic on scene as the sole first responder at a horrific accident where the outcome looks grim. He asks the victim as they are awaiting assistance, "Do you believe in God, Steven?" The man shakes his head and says, "No. I mean … I don't know." Bobby gently continues, "Well, I can promise you this—Jesus wants to know you. He loves you and he suffered and died on the cross so we could be forgiven." "Forgiven?" the man asks. "Absolutely. If you believe and accept Jesus Christ as your Savior." Steven, now struggling to speak, manages to utter, "Jesus. Please forgive me. I'm sorry. So sorry."

Throughout the history of the church and the establishment of many different denominations inside the overarching belief of Christianity, the language of salvation has been hotly debated, creating many dividing lines among Jesus' followers. From the words spoken to the prayers prayed indicating a desire to begin a relationship with God through Christ, these areas have been scrutinized by countless theologians over a myriad of reasons.

There is an amazing story in Scripture that strikingly resembles our featured scene today. Christ is on the cross, hanging between two thieves. He is innocent of all wrong-doing, while the two men on each side are guilty of all charges. Let's look at the exchange that occurred between the three:

> One of the criminals hanging beside him scoffed, "So you're the Messiah, are you? Prove it by saving yourself—and us, too, while you're at it!" But the other criminal protested. 'Don't you even fear God when you are dying? We deserve to die for our evil deeds, but this man hasn't done one thing wrong." Then he said, "Jesus, remember me when you come into your Kingdom." And Jesus replied, "Today you will be with me in Paradise. This is a solemn promise." —Luke 23:39–43 TLB

In these few verses, we find the two extreme responses mankind has made regarding Jesus throughout history. One against versus one for; one rejecting versus one accepting; one relying on self versus one relying on God. Jesus, on the cross in between, is dying for both, making the choice available to all.

The first man was condescending, angry, and sarcastic. His bitter words were threatening and, most importantly, disbelieving. The second man was humbled, repentant, and amazingly defensive of Jesus' innocence. But a most fascinating thought recorded here was likely the second man's final words. He called Jesus by name. He expressed great faith by stating Jesus would most certainly be returning to heaven. The thief didn't even actually ask for salvation as much as he simply requested to be remembered. Another way to view his statement might be: "Jesus, please don't forget about me when you return to your kingdom."

Jesus' reply was a definitive promise from God himself. When did he say the man would not only be remembered, but be with him? Today! And where would he be supernaturally transported with Jesus? Heaven. What an amazing exchange of belief and hope. The finite met the infinite; the lost was found—in a simple sentence.

We must also take Jesus' lack of response to the first man as a definitive answer. That thief chose his own way, mocking God, so Jesus allowed him his freedom to choose. Jesus didn't respond or defend himself, but rather focused on the one who did express belief.

In your days of doubt—and we shall all have them—remind yourself of the thief who humbly asked for Jesus to remember him. Let these verses be a comfort to your faith. While your prayer asking Christ for salvation may have been somewhat different than the man in the accident or the thief on the cross, we must realize the intent of the heart is more important than the choice of wording. The proper phrase does not save—Jesus does! There is no magic formula, but there is a merciful Father.

Whether "Remember me" or "Jesus, I'm so sorry," God is focused on the attitude of the heart. He is constantly seeking to save the lost (Luke 19:10).

In your journal today, finish these thoughts:

If I encountered Steven today, just as Bobby did, I would tell him …

Jesus, I believe you saved me, because on my day of salvation, I prayed …

I'm so very sorry Lord for not coming to You sooner. Please forgive me & come into my heart. I want to live for You from now on. ♡

HEAR HERE

Throughout the Gospels, we read a consistent and repetitive statement Jesus makes while teaching. The words seemed to be a "go-to phrase" for him: "Whoever has ears to hear, let them hear" (NIV).

Jesus didn't say, "he that has ears," because that would be most everyone. He specifically said, "ears to hear." Jesus knew that whether it was 500 people gathered on a hillside, fifty by the lakeside, or five at a dinner table, not everyone would …

… care to hear what he had to say.

… understand what he had to say.

… act on what he had to say.

Jesus knew his real audience was always a minority of the majority; a small group inside the congregation; those who were ready versus those who would resist. He knew not everyone was a potential disciple. Some already had their minds made up. Some couldn't overcome their own hearts. But there were always a few who had ears to hear—who cared, understood, and acted upon what he said.

People haven't really changed much since then, have they? And Jesus is *still* speaking to the minority of the majority; the small group inside the congregation; those who are ready versus those who resist. It is just as true today—there are those who hear and take action.

J.D. and Teri are a seasoned couple that have endured much life and heartache. Time has taken a toll on them with some cynicism and passivity creeping in over the years. Back at home, after hearing Pastor Matthew's message about the cross, J.D. shares with conviction, "Remember how Matthew said belief is an action? Well, it's time for us to act." Teri, not quite ready yet to have ears to hear, responds with, "You're telling me you're turning our whole life upside down because of a sermon?" J.D. presses on, "No. I've been thinking about it for a long time. But his sermon's given me the courage to actually do something about it."

Note that Teri said "our whole life," but J.D. responded with "I" and "me." He knew he was convicted but placed no pressure on her. He was allowing for the fact that her heart hadn't yet heard, but he was confident his had.

One who also had ears to hear was the disciple Peter. After Jesus ascended to heaven and the Holy Spirit had come, we find him in Acts 2 preaching before thousands. The same man who had denied Jesus before a few people during the trials was exalting him boldly before great crowds. One of the first sentences of his message was, "Listen carefully to what I say." After his message was given, evidently many were listening intently and had "ears to hear."

> Those who believed what he said were baptized. There were about 3,000 more followers added that day.
> —Acts 2:41 NLV

Some in the crowd who responded to Peter may have seen or heard Jesus before, or at least heard about him, and then Peter's sermon gave them "the courage to actually do something about it," to bring back J.D.'s words. These people were given the opportunity to hear and believe that Jesus was indeed Messiah, Lord, and Savior.

Here's the amazing connection between today's Scripture and Teri's struggling question—three thousand people really did turn their "whole lives upside down because of a sermon!" A sermon given about true belief.

Today, while you may never stand before thousands to preach, you will talk to countless people who desperately need the truth—the truth you hold in your heart. Be encouraged that, while there will always be some who will resist and reject, there will also be those who …

… care to hear what you have to say.

… understand what you have to say.

… act on what you have to say.

God wants to involve you in reaching the people he loves. Go ahead. Turn someone's life upside down. After all, as Pastor Matthew said, "Belief is an action."

In your journal, write down the names of those people in your life you believe may be ready to hear. Write out ways you can believe and take action—for their sake.

THE HOLE TRUTH

Pastor Matthew's headlights shine on Malachi, suddenly illuminating the man and his message. The grizzled and weary African American street preacher is carrying an eight-foot cross on his shoulder as he steps in front of the pastor's car. The traffic light turns green and Matthew waits for Malachi to move on, but he doesn't. It's more than a little intimidating as the preacher holding the cross announces, "Whole world's runnin' to its destruction. Devil's dug a big hole and people are fightin' each other for the chance to be first to jump in."

As we consume the daily news feed and scan an endless stream of social media, one thing seems certain—our world is not going in the right direction. And it's going there fast. We completely understand Malachi's declaration and accurate analogy. War, disease, famine, corruption, cruelty, and even brutality in the name of religion are ravaging the global landscape, recognizing no borders.

God's enemy, Satan, has initiated an effective strategy for making destructive lifestyles look increasingly appealing to the masses. The saturation of seduction slowly desensitizes the minds and eventually the hearts of millions. The "hole," as Malachi dubbed it, has indeed created a battle to reach the bottom.

As followers of Jesus, all the bad news can cause us to forget God has already won the war. We must remember we are simply living in the space between Christ's resurrection and second coming. God used the cross to defeat the enemy and offer us hope. While he said the world would get worse, his promises constantly remind us of the final victory, as well as the abundant life we may live amidst the chaos.

Paul expressed this well in his letter to the Philippians:

> I often warned you that many people are living as enemies of the cross of Christ. And now with tears in my eyes, I warn you again that they are headed for hell! They worship their stomachs and brag about the disgusting things they do. All they can think about are the things of this world. But we are citizens of heaven and are eagerly waiting for our Savior to come from there. —Philippians 3:18–20 CEV

There is a stark similarity between Paul's warning here and Malachi's commentary on mankind. The apostle's analogy of man's insatiable appetite for satisfying self and boasting about the outcome rings true even today. His language regarding "the things of this world" was not speaking of our everyday lives, but rather the self-centered, sensuous, and sexually driven actions that worldly living glorifies.

Paul reminded the church of their current residence and ultimate destination in the kingdom of God. We must keep this same mind-set in the forefront of all we do. Let's face it—the constant battle for the balance of "being in the world but not of it" is a tough walk. Here are a few points of encouragement for today:

1: People need to see God's love and grace, not our disapproval and disgust. After all, though Christians are forgiven and redeemed, we are *all* still sinners.

2: We must be extensions of God's grace to those around us. Most testimonies of those who come to Christ speak of grace shown by someone and freedom expressed.

3: Allow God to convict; we don't condemn.

The hole to which Malachi referred? God, through his Spirit, will bring conviction in his time, in his way, for someone to ask for help in getting out. Our condemnation can only hinder God's activity and ruin the relationship.

Is there an attitude toward a person or people that you need to change with God's help?

Is there a relationship in your life where the person desperately needs to be shown grace and love?

Is there somewhere you need patience to allow for God's conviction?

If you are a citizen of heaven, then you know there is plenty of room in the neighborhood for those who believe.

In your journal, complete these sentences.
Father, please change my attitude about …
Father, please give me the grace for …
Father, help me to show I am a citizen of heaven by …

VOICE LESSONS

G-Ma, Pretty Boy's and Kriminal's endearing nickname for their grandmother, looks over at Pretty Boy and says, "Come on over here." He moves closer and sits beside her, as she's probably the only person he feels safe with right now. G-Ma has no idea that Pretty Boy's world has come crashing down and fear has gripped his heart like a vise. He looks at her like he may never see her again.

G-Ma takes his face in her hands and speaks softly and lovingly, "My pretty boy. Think back for a minute to those nights when I'd sing you to sleep. Every night, the same song." She begins to sing a few lines of an old gospel hymn entitled "Seek Ye First." Pretty Boy's eyes well up with tears from the sound of the familiar words that echo back to a more innocent and carefree time in his life. G-Ma finishes the chorus, then looks her grandson right in the eye. "I know it ain't easy for you out there. You got voices pulling you in all different directions. But there's only one voice that matters." She places her hand over his heart and gently speaks, "You listen for that and you follow it. And you'll be just fine."

Pretty Boy knew what it meant to hear a lot of voices telling you what to do. He needed desperately to hear some truth above the noise of the world.

Consider your own voices. Spouse. Roommate. Children. Bosses. Employees. Business connections. Extended family. Neighbors. Friends. Church staff. All voices we know well. Some we love. Some we like. Some, not so much. Oftentimes we can feel as though they are all talking at once. Pressure, expectations, and demands mount.

This makes hearing God an even bigger challenge. One of the greatest spiritual disciplines we can learn is how to hear the voice of God. Whether in a room filled with silence or a crowded space, we must listen for his Spirit to speak to our hearts. God taught the prophet Elijah an interesting lesson in listening while he was in the middle of nowhere, completely alone:

> "Go out and stand before me on the mountain," the Lord told him. And as Elijah stood there, the Lord passed by, and a mighty windstorm hit the mountain. It was such a terrible blast that the rocks were torn loose, but the Lord was not in the wind. After the wind there was an earthquake, but the Lord was not in the earthquake. And after the earthquake there was a fire, but the Lord was not in the fire. And after the fire there was the sound of a gentle whisper. When Elijah heard it, he wrapped his face in his cloak and went out and stood at the entrance of the cave.
> —1 Kings 19:11–13 NLT

Amidst the wrath of three forces of nature, Elijah waited and finally heard God whisper through the silence. Elijah discerned where God's voice was—and where it wasn't. He knew what he heard, and he heard what he knew.

Here are a few practical tips for discerning the difference between your own voice and God's:

You may be hearing your own voice when …

… you only hear your usual concerns, fears, and plans.

… your normal chaotic thoughts are connected.

… you hear word-by-word familiar lines.

You may be hearing God's voice when a thought …

… comes suddenly, like seeing an entire painting unveiled all at once.

… is accompanied by great peace that overcomes any fear.

… lines up uncompromisingly with the truth of Scripture.

While these certainly are not foolproof, consider how they apply to your own heart. No one can better discern God's patterns of communication to your own spirit than you. Time and experience with him are the best indicators to know his will for your life.

Today, consider prayerfully where you are hearing his gentle whisper … then listen and obey, just as G-Ma said.

In your journal, complete these thoughts:

Lord, the noise in my life today is …

Lord, I need to hear your whisper today about …

CROSSROADS

It is nighttime in Chicago. Ahead, we see a light piercing through the darkness. The closer we get, we can see that the object standing out from the pitch black of evening is a large cross affixed prominently on the top of a church building. And not just any church, but Pastor Matthew's. We hear him speak …

"See that cross? Countless people pass underneath it every day. But how many notice it, and for those who do, what does it mean to them? Ask me and I'll tell you it's about forgiveness and redemption. Because I know that's what it's supposed to mean. But what does it really mean and why do we all seem to forget it? And how might God—assuming there is a God—go about trying to get us to remember?"

It is early morning, just a few miles outside Jerusalem. Two men are talking while they walk to a village called Emmaus. Seemingly out of nowhere, another man walks up, joining them on the road. He asks, "What are you discussing so intently as you walk along?" One of the men, Cleopas, stops in his tracks, apparently troubled and not up for small talk. He sarcastically answers, "You must be the only person in Jerusalem who hasn't heard about all the things that have happened there the last few days." "What things?" the stranger asks. "The things that happened to Jesus, the man from Nazareth," the other man answers.

The two men then proceed to explain about Jesus' miracles and teaching, and then his trial and crucifixion. They go on to express disappointment that he must have only been a prophet who died, because they had hoped he was the Messiah to rescue Israel.

The stranger begins to speak, taking the men all the way back to Moses, through the prophets, and explaining to them how all of Scripture pointed to Christ. When he is done and they have arrived in Emmaus, the two men ask the stranger to come to their home, which was the custom of the day for neighborly hospitality. But as they sit down to dinner, a very mystical and miraculous moment occurs.

The man to whom they had been talking for hours now took some bread, broke it, blessed it, and handed some to them. At that moment, the men realize the stranger is Jesus! God opened their eyes to the truth (see Luke 24:13–31).

What an amazing story, that Jesus would pursue those men to be certain they found him! Two men who had missed the message of the cross became confirmed eyewitnesses. Can you imagine walking with Jesus for miles and having him explain how all the Scriptures fit together to tell of him?

The "aha moment" occurred when the men shared: "Didn't our hearts burn within us as he talked with us on the road and explained the Scriptures to us?" (Luke 24:32 NLT)

Once we truly meet Jesus and his Spirit fills our souls, making our "hearts burn within us," the cross becomes deeply personal. Jesus died for—me. The cross was intended for—me, but he took my place. How can we possibly forget such a gift?

There are people all around you who don't yet know what the cross means. That is where you come in.

Something deep in every person's soul cries out for an explanation of how they fit into this grand plan called life. Just as Jesus walked up and engaged the two men in conversation, then explained himself to them after hearing their concerns, we too can tell others about his life in us.

Here is a very simple way to share your faith, your own story of what the cross means to you. In three to four sentences for each point, share …

… what your life was like before Christ.

… the circumstances of how you came to know Jesus.

… how a relationship with Jesus changed your life.

… something God is currently doing in your life today.

In your journal, write out your own testimony using these four points. Writing it down and rehearsing it a few times will make you prepared for "walking down the road with Jesus."

MAKE A
RIGHT TURN

Samantha is grateful Joe allowed her and her daughter, Lily, to stay in his home, though she has no idea where he went the night before so as to make them feel comfortable and safe. Samantha begins telling Joe how she and Lily ended up homeless. She closes with, "Not the way I thought things would end up. I'll tell you that." Joe has listened intently, but now he wants to encourage her. "Hey, it's not over yet," he states. "Take it from someone who knows. Things can turn around. God has a way of making bad things turn out good." Samantha just gives a shrug, turning her eyes downward, as her countenance falls. Joe seems surprised, "What? You don't believe?"

In what seemed like just a matter of minutes, Joseph's crazy, roller coaster of a life had just taken yet another wild turn. After standing before Pharaoh and interpreting his dreams, Joseph explained that seven years of abundance would be followed by seven years of famine. After hearing him out, the great ruler of Egypt decided on his best plan of action for the nation.

> The king said to Joseph, "God has shown you all this, so it is obvious that you have greater wisdom

and insight than anyone else. I will put you in charge of my country, and all my people will obey your orders. Your authority will be second only to mine."
—Genesis 41:39–40 GNT

Let's rewind and list some facts about Joseph's life to better understand this moment.

He was the favored son of his father among many brothers.

His father gave him a very special coat.

His jealous brothers decided to get rid of him.

They stripped him of his coat and sold him to traders as a slave.

They told Dad he was killed by a wild animal.

Potiphar, an officer of the king, bought Joseph as a slave.

Potiphar placed Joseph in charge of his entire household.

Potiphar's wife attempted to seduce Joseph.

Joseph refused her, and she accused him of attempted rape.

Joseph went to prison for years.

Pharaoh heard that Joseph had successfully interpreted dreams and called for him.

This series of events took place from around the time Joseph was seventeen to the time he was thirty. He spent his last few teenage years and all of his twenties in slavery or prison!

There are many times in Joseph's life when he could have echoed Samantha's words, "Not the way I thought things would end up. I'll tell you that." But then Joseph certainly could relate to Joe's statement of faith as well: "Take it from someone who knows. Things can turn around. God has a way of making bad things turn out good."

The key to the ups and downs of Joseph's life, as well as what Joe was working on in his life, is found in Genesis 39:2, with a slightly different version in 39:23: "The Lord was with Joseph and made him successful" (GNT).

In our wealth- and fame-crazed culture, we certainly wouldn't define anything about Joseph's life as successful until the final chapter, but here we see success to God is defined as one who is faithful and obedient to him. No matter where God placed Joseph, from prison to palace, he displayed the same character.

It would also seem fitting that in Joseph's life, he would be found saying to others who shrugged off the idea of a good God, "What? You don't believe?"

In closing, here is both a maturity test and a reality check for us all. Do we celebrate when times are great, but complain when they go south? Does our attitude have a sliding scale dependent on how we view our surroundings? Are we good with God when he blesses, but doubt him when he seems to be silent?

Do you believe the Lord is with you? You should, because he is.

Do you believe he has made you successful by his definition? If not, you can be, just like Joseph and Joe.

In your journal, finish these sentences with your own words:

I know the Lord is with me because …

I believe God has made me successful, because I am blessed with …

IF THERE
WERE NO IFS

J esus was walking amidst a crowd when a man called out that his son was possessed by a spirit that made him mute and caused severe seizures. When they brought the boy to him, the demonic spirit responded to being in the presence of Jesus by throwing the boy to the ground and convulsing.

> Jesus asked the boy's father, "How long has he been like this?" "From childhood," he answered. "It has often thrown him into fire or water to kill him. But if you can do anything, take pity on us and help us." "'If you can'"? said Jesus. "Everything is possible for one who believes." Immediately the boy's father exclaimed, "I do believe; help me overcome my unbelief!"
> —Mark 9:21–24 NIV

Jesus rebuked the spirit and it left the boy, thereby restoring him to complete health and freedom. There are two quite fascinating points to Jesus' dialogue with the dad.

First, the boy's situation didn't faze Christ at all. His focus was completely on the man's comment about belief, or maybe more accurately, lack of it.

Second, Jesus doesn't show offense about the comment, but rather places the focus back on the person who believes.

The point we want to zero in on today, however, is verse 24, where the father says, "I do believe; help me overcome my unbelief!" What a great phrase for all Christ-followers to hang on to. While this might appear at first read to be a negative statement, there is much truth and a great prayer in the spirit of these words. First, we focus on his first three words: *I do believe*! But then he readily admits he needs growth and maturity to believe at a deeper level. This will always be true of us at any point of spiritual maturity until we get to heaven.

It is unlike any other kind of growth we can experience in this life. Let's look closer at this concept ...

Spiritual growth is like a plant. You can take a look at any plant of any type and make a judgment call on whether it is thriving or dying. The appearance of the leaves, branches, or blooms gives us clues. Is it reaching upward, showing health and growth, or wilting downward in distress? But is a plant ever just in a state of neutrality, not growing or dying? No, it is always heading in one direction or the other. The same is true for our spiritual growth.

The people around us know if we are growing or wilting in our maturity. Going forward or falling backward. Our level of belief versus unbelief is usually more visible than we even realize. A great question we should ask regularly is: Am I growing spiritually?

Spiritual growth is not measured by seniority, but by maturity. Likely right now, you can think of someone who claims to have been a Christian for many years, yet you wouldn't count on that person for spiritual wisdom or help. You see years of religious activity, but few moments of spiritual maturity.

On the other hand, you likely know someone who has been a Christian for a relatively short time, and this person's fervor draws you to his or her faith. Their maturity is showing and growing at a rapid pace. You can literally see it. The time this person is putting into prayer, Bible study, discipleship, and fellowship is creating growth.

But the great news is a wilting person can become a growing person at any time. Surrender to Christ is the key—saying, "I do believe. Help me overcome my unbelief." Between our salvation and entrance to heaven, our goal is to increase belief and decrease unbelief.

In his message about the cross, Pastor Matthew states, "What does it mean to believe? I remember hearing once that true belief is an action. So if we believe that Christ died for us, it should bring us not just to our knees, but to our feet."

In your journal, write down at least one step you can take to bring your faith to action, to help unbelief in your life become belief.

TRAITORS TO TRANSLATORS

The police are closing in on the church parking lot where Pretty Boy has run looking for cover. The lights are on inside, so he quietly opens the door and slips through. To his surprise, he is staring at a church service in progress. He can't go back outside, so he's committed. As he walks toward the back row of pews, he hears, "There's a seat for you up there." It's Joe, who's serving as a greeter tonight. Pretty Boy mutters, "I'm not staying." Joe, who has seen this scenario many times before, offers back, "I think you should."

Joe nods subtly toward the police flashlights outside, now visible from the doors. Pretty Boy, in his usual defensive posture, launches back, "You don't know me." Joe, undeterred, says firmly, "Sure I do. I been where you're going and believe me—the only way out you're ever gonna find is right in here." He nods toward the church full of people.

Saul was still talking much about how he would like to kill the followers of the Lord. He went to the head religious leader. He asked for letters to be written to the Jewish places of worship in the city of Damascus. The letters were to say that if he found any men or women

63

following the Way of Christ he might bring them to Jerusalem in chains.

He went on his way until he came near Damascus. All at once he saw a light from heaven shining around him. He fell to the ground. Then he heard a voice say, "Saul, Saul, why are you working so hard against Me?" Saul answered, "Who are You, Lord?" He said, "I am Jesus, the One Whom you are working against. You hurt yourself by trying to hurt Me." —Acts 9:1–5 NLV

While Pretty Boy was the one being pursued by the law and Saul was the pursuer of Christians, even still, both were running from Jesus. G-Ma raised Pretty Boy with her faith as an anchor, so he had heard the truth. Saul was a religious leader, zealous to stamp out what he believed to be a threat to the belief he held so tightly. But both men were miles away from God until he drew them to the place to be confronted by him. Joe was the doorway God used to help connect Pretty Boy to his roots. Jesus himself met Saul.

Jesus, now post resurrection, asked an intriguing question of Saul. Christ asked why he was working against him and trying to hurt him! This was personal.

As we read on in Acts 9, no one else saw Jesus on the road that day but Saul. He was struck blind for three days and told to go to Damascus to await further instructions. He did just as he was told. His murderous, rage-filled days were over. The encounter on the road radically changed his life from that moment on. But we must always remind ourselves that the man who is responsible for the bulk of the New Testament started out as a cruel murderer. Why? Because only God will change traitors into translators.

In TV and movies, the hero searches desperately to catch the treacherous villain. We all know what is going to happen in the end, no matter how many car chases, shoot-outs, and foot races we watch. The hero will catch the bad guy, and he will either be a) killed, or b) manhandled, then sent to prison forever. We wouldn't feel vindicated in our viewing if one of those two scenarios didn't play out.

God, however, goes after a traitor, pursues him or her, then upon the capture of the heart, tells the person, "Now go. Translate my love to a lost and dying world." That is exactly what Jesus did with Paul. That is exactly what Joe knew God could do with Pretty Boy, because God had done the exact same thing for him.

In your journal, write down a few of the ways Jesus has come after you. Then list some ways you can translate Christ to a lost world. What skill, talent, gift, or passion can God use as you surrender it to him?

LIFE SAVING 101

Several years ago, a certain celebrity began displaying extreme behavior and was making the news on a daily basis with some very strange quotes. The media began a feeding frenzy, clamoring to be the first to report what the star was saying each day. Promotional companies began selling T-shirts with his soon-infamous quotes emblazoned on them. But anyone who has seen the dangers of addiction before could tell there was something very wrong going on.

A few months after his life settled down and the media had turned their attention toward others, the celebrity appeared without fanfare on a late-night talk show. The host asked him the question, "So, will you, can you, ever go through this again?" His answer was humble, as he stated, "I can't. Don't have the energy. I'm all out of slogans."

The truth is we all have our "slogans," and we use them until they don't work anymore. Because we are all ruled by our sin nature, it often takes us having to come to the end of ourselves before we truly see the need for God in our lives. We are fooled into thinking we have the resources, intellect, skill, and power within to solve any problem ... until we can't. We're faced with the sudden death or illness of a loved one;

a marriage we can't fix; a child we can't control; a business we can't bail out; or a debt too big to repay. When something finally gets bigger than us, we give up. And look for someone bigger than the problems. When we hit bottom and can only look up, we see the end of ourselves and where God begins.

In Jesus' teaching, he explained to us how we can avoid hitting bottom and how to grab all of life, as he always meant us to live.

> Jesus then told the crowd and the disciples to come closer, and he said: "If any of you want to be my followers, you must forget about yourself. You must take up your cross and follow me. If you want to save your life, you will destroy it. But if you give up your life for me and for the good news, you will save it. What will you gain, if you own the whole world but destroy yourself? What could you give to get back your soul?"
> —Mark 8:34–37 CEV

When we read these verses in today's context, we can easily miss the great shock a person would have experienced hearing Jesus talk of how to save your life. The cross was the most torturous execution in that day. Telling a group of people they must "take up their cross" is like telling a church congregation today that they must "climb up into the electric chair to save your life." Or "crawl up onto the gurney and administer the lethal injection to save your life." Of course, Jesus was not telling everyone to literally take up a cross the way he did. The concept of dying to self and giving control fully to God is the true point of this teaching. Admit you're all out of slogans.

Pastor Matthew reaches into his pocket and pulls out a little wooden cross. "I challenge all of you tonight to carry this cross with you. Let it be a reminder of the gift Christ gave to us. Let it inspire you to live your life as Jesus lived." He holds up the small cross and continues, "For this is not just a symbol, not just an idea. It's truth. And if you believe that truth, then let your actions show it."

Hitting bottom and looking up changes you. Your actions must then reflect your willingness to change. Realizing you no longer have all the answers humbles you. Your actions must then reflect your willingness to let go of pride. Admitting you're all out of slogans makes you look for real answers. Your actions must then reflect your willingness to seek wisdom beyond your own.

Is there a place in your life where you've hit bottom, no longer know what to do, and are fresh out of answers, all out of slogans? Confess those to God today by writing them down in your journal. Talk to Jesus about them and then let your actions show you're serious about change.

PROVIDENTIAL PLOT TWISTS

The service ends and Pretty Boy is still sitting right where he landed for what now seems like an eternity ago. Something about the stillness and peace of the church makes it feel like, well … a sanctuary to him. He hasn't sensed anything like this in a very long time.

"Why'd you do it?" he asks Joe, referring to how Joe didn't alert the police to his whereabouts. "Do what?" Joe asks. "You know," Pretty Boy states. Joe pauses a moment, then decides to be straight with him. "The Holy Spirit put it on my heart that you were in trouble and asked me to help you." The gang member pops back, "You expect me to believe that?!" Joe firmly offers, "Doesn't matter if you do or if you don't. You're still here, aren't you?"

Pretty Boy senses a strange need to stay right where he is. Joe asks, "You okay?" "Yeah. I'm just thinkin'," he responds. Joe gives a knowing smile and says, "Tends to happen when the Spirit gets involved."

In Acts 8, there is an account of the disciple Philip being directed by the Spirit to walk down the road from Jerusalem to Gaza. He came upon an Ethiopian eunuch, an official in charge of the treasury, on his way home in his chariot. Philip saw that he was reading a scroll of the book of Isaiah. The Spirit directed Philip to the man. As he ran up beside the chariot, he asked, "Do you understand what you're reading?" The eunuch "just happened" to be reading a passage of prophecy about Jesus.

> The eunuch asked Philip, "Was Isaiah talking about himself or someone else?" So Philip began with this same Scripture and then used many others to tell him about Jesus. As they rode along, they came to a small body of water, and the eunuch said, "Look! Water! Why can't I be baptized?" "You can," Philip answered, "if you believe with all your heart." And the eunuch replied, "I believe that Jesus Christ is the Son of God." He stopped the chariot, and they went down into the water and Philip baptized him. —Acts 8:34–38 TLB

The timing of Pretty Boy coming in the back of the church with Joe greeting, and Philip coming up to the eunuch's chariot, shows the way the Holy Spirit can orchestrate divine intersections between people.

The Holy Spirit, the third member of the Trinity or the Godhead, creates some quite amazing and miraculous moments. Here are just a few circumstances to watch for in your own life.

Holy Coincidence

Everything has a purpose inside God's plan. When something in your life looks like an incredible coincidence, start looking at every angle, because God is doing something. Don't miss it; something good is happening or about to happen. God uses everything; nothing is wasted.

Divine Appointment

So many people's testimonies tell of a relationship, meeting, or occurrence of some kind that intersects lives at just the right time for an eternal purpose. We hear phrases such as, "had it been any other hour that day, we would not have met," or "I was delayed in leaving and couldn't understand why, but then," or "she felt God tell her someone would need this when she arrived." Every day, we should watch for divine appointments he has planned for us to touch people in our path, just like Philip with the eunuch.

Righteous Interruption

Does God have the freedom to interrupt your life, like he did Philip's, knowing you'll respond? Of course, he knows your schedule and your responsibilities to work within those, but if he really is the Lord of your life, his Spirit should be allowed to alter your plans for his purposes. Listen for righteous interruptions.

There is no question you will be blessed every time you hear God's Spirit and obey his voice. Joe would have rather been on the second row during the service, but he knew he needed to be greeting that night. Philip may not have had a trip to Gaza planned that day, but by that evening he and an Ethiopian official were glad he listened.

Write down in your journal the story of your last holy coincidence, divine appointment, or righteous interruption.

GETTING GUILT
GONE FOR GOOD

After dropping J.D. and Teri off safely at home, Pastor Matthew starts retracing his route to look for the wayward pregnant girl he passed walking in the wrong neighborhood. He can't shake off what he saw. Soon, he notices a figure beside a dumpster. Her name is Maggie. The pastor stops the car and calls out, "Are you okay?" She stops and gives him an "Are you kidding me?" look. "Just peachy," she answers sarcastically, going back to searching the dumpster for food.

Undeterred, Matthew says, "Look, I know you don't know me, but is there anything you need?" Maggie, now suspicious of the motives of any and all men, asks, "What are you? Some kind of freak?" "No," he responds. "Just someone who wants to help." After a moment of uncertainty, considering her desperate circumstances, Maggie agrees to allow Matthew to help her.

For the vast majority of people today, life seems to only get busier. Demands come at us from every direction. People make statements such as, "I just wish I had more hours in a day" and "I'm not sure how I'm going to find the time to do everything I need to get done."

If you then mix being a Christian who wants to solve the

problems of the world with the constant time crunch of life, the lack of available hours just begins to create guilt and frustration. We drive by a homeless person, feel compassion, look at the time, and then keep driving. Guilt. We think this is the year we're going to help a needy family at Christmas. Then on December 26, we realize we missed it again. The crazy schedule collides with the needs of the world, and we feel overwhelmed, at times helpless.

The old saying, "Nothing changes if nothing changes" certainly comes to mind here. We also remember the definition of insanity: "Doing the same thing over and over again, expecting different results every time." But here's a more encouraging saying on which we can focus: "The world is changed by those who show up."

Take a look at James's sobering take on this dilemma:

> What good is it, dear brothers and sisters, if you say you have faith but don't show it by your actions? Can that kind of faith save anyone? Suppose you see a brother or sister who has no food or clothing, and you say, "Good-bye and have a good day; stay warm and eat well"—but then you don't give that person any food or clothing. What good does that do?
> —James 2:14–16 NLT

James is, in effect, saying that as followers of Jesus we must show up and change *someone's* world. Well wishes and good intentions won't help people; only action will.

Here are a few tips to end the guilt and get involved:

1: Find and focus on **one** ***issue in*** **one** ***area.*** Don't get overwhelmed by the magnitude of the masses. The reason child sponsorship has been so well received from hunger-relief organizations is it puts one face on famine. People think, *I can't solve world hunger, but I can help feed* this *child.* Put a face and a name to the problems of the world by helping one person or one situation.

2: Match your gifts and skills to ministry needs. If you love to cook, feed hungry people. If you're a handyman, fix broken things in someone's broken home. If you're an accountant, offer to do the taxes for the single moms in your church. If you can hug a child, help in the nursery. See the connection? Something you can do can be shared with someone to become a ministry.

3: End the guilt; give it to God. God doesn't want his children to feel guilty; he wants to use us to "go." Serve. Love. Make disciples. The next time you are faced with a person in need, go do what God has empowered you to do.

Finish these sentences in your journal:
God, I often feel guilty about …
The gift or skill I could give to help people is …
Lord, help me to let go of guilt today and be a go-er by …

ABOUT TIME
FOR ABOUT-FACE

The Bible says in Romans 6:23, 'for the wages of sin is death.' And because we are all sinful, that's a death we deserve," Pastor Matthew shares with conviction in his message, as we have come to expect from him.

Because God is holy, he has one standard, one plumb line drawn across mankind. One sin + one time = death. That is exactly where the old adage originates, "The ground is level at the foot of the cross." No "levels" of sin exist with God. Someone can't be "better" than someone else when all have fallen and failed. Holiness can't allow for any sin—neither doing the wrong thing nor omitting the right thing.

Pastor Matthew continues his message …

"But the cross promises us a way out—the only way out. When you come to the cross, you come by way of repentance. And repentance means to change the way you live. To turn from your sins and turn to Christ. The cross of Jesus Christ says, 'I will save you. I will forgive you. I will give you new life.' Romans 10:13 states, 'for, "Everyone who calls on the name of the Lord will be saved'" (NIV).

The simple definition of the Greek word from which we translate the word *repentance* is "about-face." A soldier is marching one direction, hears the command, turns around, and goes in the opposite direction.

There is an aspect of physics applied in the spirit of this word as well. When you turn around and walk *away* from something—sin—you are then walking *toward* something else—Christ. This solution to our problem of separation from God gives us a reason to "about-face." We turn from our sin and death and walk toward his grace and life.

As Pastor Matthew said in his message, the cross offers a way out, the only way out. Many people today criticize the statement that there is only one way to God; they call Christianity "narrow-minded" for expressing this truth.

Imagine you are in a crowded building. Suddenly, flames are shooting all around and smoke is filling the air. Fire! Everyone begins to search for the many doors leading out of the building but quickly realizes the flames are threatening any escape. Finally, a man calls out, "Everyone! Head this way! It's our only way out!" Only one door is a right-of-way to safety; all other options lead to death. A few people hear and respond, running to safety. But the majority of the people begin to protest, "Who is he to say that is the only way out? I know for a fact there are more doors that could be options to get to safety. In fact, I feel that any way we choose to go out, no matter how many flames are blocking the way, those should surely be safe paths for us to leave. We're finding our own way!"

Ridiculous? Yes. Would that happen in the panic of a fire? Of course not. Everyone would run toward safety. But isn't that exactly the argument of multiple ways to salvation? Many just don't realize the building is on fire until it is too late or their chosen path only led to destruction.

There is another point in Scripture that is equally as clear: "For everyone who calls on the name of the Lord shall be saved." Everyone who repents is saved! No one refused. The ground is indeed level at the foot of the cross!

In your journal, complete these thoughts:

Father, today I need your help to walk away from …
Father, today help me walk toward …

HEAVENLY HELP
FOR HYPOCRITES

W ell, how about you don't let it ruin your dinner ... or mine," Andrea quips, after Dr. Farell has expressed his frustration in seeing a nurse from the hospital and her husband praying before their meal at a high-end restaurant in which they are dining.

The doctor continues, "I'm just sick of it. I save their lives, and who do they wake up thanking?" In a disrespectful manner, he mocks, "Thank you, Jesus. Thank you, Lord." Andrea responds, "Hey, no argument here. I grew up with *those* people. They're a bunch of hypocrites. I just never realized you had such a God complex."

Farell continues firmly, "It's not a complex. I do his work. I should get the credit."

The simple definition of a hypocrite is one who says to do one thing and then does another. Words and actions don't match. A hypocrite is consistently inconsistent. We are all hypocrites. Morally, spiritually, and even intellectually, we are consistently inconsistent.

In our daily lives as Christ-followers, we encounter three groups of people:

*1: **The brother and sister in Christ.*** These are the people who have a relationship with Christ and we can see the fruit of their lives as we live in their midst. From this group, we gain community, identity, and fellowship. Inside this group, we will have friendships with two segments: those more mature than us from whom we can learn, and those we can teach because we are more mature than them. This community of growing and sharing is where we derive life and strength to continue our journey in Jesus.

*2: **Those who don't yet know Christ.*** This segment of the population is actually growing in large numbers by the year. Obviously, we must always be very careful not to judge, but this is more of a discerning for the purpose of prayer and ministry to help people come to Christ. While we stay anchored in relationships with the first group, we all reach out to grow the community of Christ by sharing his life and love with those who don't yet know him.

*3: **The religious.*** These are those who have adopted any belief system outside of Christianity. Jesus regularly separated those who followed him from those who claimed a religion, as in our earlier reference to the Pharisees. While Dr. Farell didn't necessarily express a disbelief in God, his words displayed a definite belief in his own abilities to save. This group will be where most of the debates, questions, and hypocritical accusations come from—people who have made up their minds while closing their hearts. Don't try and outsmart these folks, but always outlove them.

In Revelation, God addressed the church at Laodicea in regard to the difference between faith and religion:

> I know everything you have done, and you are not cold or hot. I wish you were either one or the other. But since you are lukewarm and neither cold nor hot, I will spit you out of my mouth. You claim to be rich and successful and to have everything you need. But you don't know how bad off you are. You are pitiful, poor, blind, and naked. —Revelation 3:15–17 CEV

As Jesus often stated, there really is no middle ground. Yet, for every place this message is communicated, there are ten others expressing God's constant invitation to salvation and fellowship. Just a few verses later in Revelation 3:20, Jesus states, "Listen! I am standing and knocking at your door. If you hear my voice and open the door, I will come in and we will eat together" (CEV).

Each time someone such as Dr. Farell is bothered by a Christian or a sign of faith, it might actually be a tug from the Holy Spirit to see the truth.

Finish these sentences in your journal:
Jesus, the believer in my life I most want to be like is …
Jesus, the person I most want to see come to know you is …
Jesus, the "lukewarm" person I am most concerned about is …

Take a moment to write out why you feel the way you do about these three people's spiritual state and then pray for each one.

No Fractions in Faith

You can stand at a window on a wintry, blustery day and watch everything being blown about. You can't see the wind or the cold, but you can see its effects. But then you walk outside. Suddenly, you've gone from observance to experience. You feel the cold. You feel the wind. The invisible power cuts through you with a deep chill.

Trying to explain to someone what a relationship with God is like is very much the same as explaining what the wind feels like to someone who has never been outside. You can't physically see God, but you can feel his effect on your soul and experience his work in your life.

Carlos and Lacey had literally just met in the middle of the night through the strangest of circumstances. Feeling they should explore this newfound friendship somehow, somewhere, they go to an all-night coffee shop. Carlos is holding the small wooden cross in his hand that his sister, Elena, gave him when he left their home. He's nervously flipping it between his fingers. Lacey can't help but notice and asks, "Are you some kind of religious nut?" "Hardly," Carlos answers, almost amused. "I got it from my sister. Her husband got himself saved a couple years back. And Elena? I guess she's about half saved. Maybe five-eighths?" Lacey responds, "I'm not sure it works that way." "It doesn't," Carlos says, now more thoughtful, "which is sort of the point."

Salvation by God's grace has always been, is, and will forever be difficult for humans to understand with our natural minds.

One night under the cover of darkness, a Pharisee named Nicodemus found Jesus to ask him questions about who he was and what he had been teaching. It was obvious he wanted to understand more, but he didn't want his fellow teachers of the law to know he was coming to Jesus.

Nicodemus called Jesus a rabbi (teacher) and confessed that he must have come from God. Take a look at their quite interesting conversation, as Nicodemus began:

> "For no one could perform the signs you are doing if God were not with him." Jesus replied, "Very truly I tell you, no one can see the kingdom of God unless they are born again." "How can someone be born when they are old?" Nicodemus asked. "Surely they cannot enter a second time into their mother's womb to be born!" Jesus answered, "Very truly I tell you, no one can enter the kingdom of God unless they are born of water and the Spirit. Flesh gives birth to flesh, but the Spirit gives birth to spirit. You should not be surprised at my saying, 'You must be born again.' The wind blows wherever it pleases. You hear its sound, but you cannot tell where it comes from or where it is going. So it is with everyone born of the Spirit." —John 3:2–8 NIV

We aren't privy to the end of the conversation or Nicodemus's response; however, it is not a stretch to imagine the Pharisee might have left with his head spinning a bit.

If you survey the Gospels, one fact is certain … there is no such thing as "half saved" or "five-eighths saved." Carlos was beginning to see the difference between his brother-in-law Bobby's commitment to Christ and his sister's. This was his way of describing her maturity and level of faith as compared to her husband. Carlos was also starting to realize that the cross is about all or none. Zero or 100 percent—no in-between.

When Christ enters our lives, no one can see this miracle occur. But, like the wind, the people around can witness the effects salvation has on our lives. They can see the wind of the Spirit blowing in us by the new attitudes, actions, and words we choose to convey. The greatest compliment of our faith happens when someone asks, "What is different about you?" This type of question is the same as saying, "I see the wind blowing. Tell me how it feels."

Finish this sentence in your journal:

Lord, if someone today were to ask me what is different about my life, I would answer by telling him or her …

THE DIVINE DIVIDING LINE

B obby is facing a serious lawsuit without the support of the city or the union, unless he signs a statement admitting he acted outside of his care mandate and apologizes for inserting his personal faith into a first-responder setting. He feels he cannot sign the statement. Elena, his wife, now upset, states, "So to prove a point, you're willing to risk everything?" Bobby responds, "I'm not trying to prove a point. I'm trying to be faithful." After more discussion, Bobby finally asks, "What do you want me to do?" Elena gives her firm ultimatum, "Sign the statement! Apologize. Do whatever they want you to."

From the first century to today, believers around the world have faced consequences ranging from outcast to execution for not renouncing their beliefs. The decision to honor God rather than man can be a heartrending and sacrificial choice.

King Nebuchadnezzar made an image of gold and placed it in Babylon. He commanded that everyone must bow down in worship when they heard the fanfare of music provided by his musicians. The alternative? Be immediately thrown into a blazing furnace.

Regardless of personal belief, people made the decision to just bow down to save their lives. But some astrologers reported to the king about these three Jewish men—Shadrach,

Meshach, and Abednego—who not only refused to bow down but also would not serve the king's gods. Enraged, Nebuchadnezzar demanded their presence. He told them the two choices again—fall down or fire up. Their response? No thanks. We will serve our God, not yours.

Nebuchadnezzar ordered the flames be made seven times hotter and his strongest soldiers to throw them in! Check out the rest of the story in Scripture:

> Suddenly King Nebuchadnezzar jumped up in alarm and said, "Didn't we throw three men, bound hand and foot, into the fire?" "That's right, O king," they said. "But look!" he said. "I see four men, walking around freely in the fire, completely unharmed! And the fourth man looks like a son of the gods!" Nebuchadnezzar went to the door of the roaring furnace and called in, "Shadrach, Meshach, and Abednego, servants of the High God, come out here!" Shadrach, Meshach, and Abednego walked out of the fire.
> —Daniel 3:24–26 MSG

Regardless of whether theologians believe an angel was with the men or Jesus himself, God provided a miraculous rescue, as well as amazing proof of his active presence with his people.

Not every story turns out like Shadrach, Meshach, and Abednego's. While this is hard for us to understand, it is also where faith must interject itself into the setting and we must trust God with the outcome. After all, for the believer, the ultimate answer is either divine help or heaven. The three men even told the king that God was their God, whether he chose to save them from the flames or not. To them, he was just as much God whether he saved them or took them to heaven.

While Bobby's situation wasn't life threatening, it is a great example of the kind of persecution that is most likely to occur in our culture today. And facing a lawsuit felt a lot like a fire to Bobby and Elena. Their lives could be destroyed nonetheless.

Bobby's statement to Elena is an awesome focal point for us today: "I'm not trying to prove a point. I'm trying to be faithful." There are those who love to make religious arguments on current issues only to appear "holy" or to sound spiritual. That is simply man trying to prove a point using God's name for cover. But when there is a clear line drawn between compromising belief and honoring God, we must put our faith to the test and believe he will help us.

Consider the choices and decisions in your own life today. While you may not be facing a lawsuit or a blazing furnace, God cares about anything you are dealing with regarding your own faith.

Complete the sentence below in your journal and then hand the situation over to God in prayer for his guidance and help.

Heavenly Father, please show me what to do today regarding …

From Fugitives to Friends

After a night in the Starlite Motel reading through the Bible he found in the nightstand drawer, Pretty Boy heads to the church where he met Joe and heard the pastor's message the night before. He walks in and sees Joe buffing a floor. After a moment of small talk, Pretty Boy asks to see the pastor, but wants Joe to stay and hear what he has to say.

Pretty Boy blurts out, "Listen, last night, this guy saved me. I mean Jesus saved me, but this guy (nodding toward Joe) was definitely part of his plan—same as you. Anyhow, when I heard you talk, I knew you were talkin' to me, even though you didn't know you were talkin' to me. What I'm tryin' to say is, I asked the Lord to save me and he did."

What a great picture of authentic belief—"I asked the Lord to save me and he did." Faith is when you know that you know you know.

Let's review—in a nutshell—the history of the world from a spiritual perspective. God created man and woman and placed them into the perfect environment. He gave them total freedom and access to him, but offered only one rule. They broke the rule and sin entered into the people, changing everything. After years of sin's effects growing worse, God decided he had

had enough and planned to flood the earth, destroying everything to start over. So with what did he choose to start over? A man with his family—Noah. While God knew sin would still be alive and well in them, he wanted to begin again with one of his original creation.

Then when God was ready to deliver the answer to sin once and for all, who did he choose to deliver his Son into the world? A woman, along with her husband, trusted to be the parents of God in the flesh. He placed trust in humans once again to deliver his salvation to the world.

Jesus came, proved his divinity time and again, died on the cross for the redemption of man, and rose from the tomb, thereby defeating sin and death for good. To whom did God then give the ministry of salvation in sharing his message with the world until he returns? Men. Women. Sinners redeemed become saints reaching out.

From day one to today, we are God's plan for reaching the world. He hands the very solution to sin back over to those who created the problem in the first place! Only God can do such a thing—turn fugitives into friends!

So what is God's plan for reaching your family, neighborhood, office, school, and the world? You. He is entrusting his message of salvation to you. It's always been Plan A. There has never been a Plan B.

All this is done by God, who through Christ changed us from enemies into his friends and gave us the task of making others his friends also. Our message is that God was making all human beings his friends

through Christ. God did not keep an account of their sins, and he has given us the message which tells how he makes them his friends. Here we are, then, speaking for Christ, as though God himself were making his appeal through us. We plead on Christ's behalf: let God change you from enemies into his friends!
—2 Corinthians 5:18–20 GNT

It's a safe guess that you have multiple job descriptions throughout your life. Spouse, parent, child, boss, employee, cook, chauffeur, handyman, financier, church member, and on and on the list goes. When we apply the message of today's passage as Christ-followers, we see that God has given us a job description that overrides many of the ones on our list and that also will be the primary responsibility that counts in heaven—that of messenger, ambassador, reconciler, and best of all—friend. He asks his friends to introduce him to their friends so he may become friends with them also. The gospel really is that simple.

Finish these sentences in your journal:

Jesus, the greatest part of my friendship with you is …
Jesus, the friend I most want to introduce to you is …
Jesus, my first responsibility I know I have from you today is to …

SAFE VERSUS CHAFE

Relationships can be some of our biggest blessings in life but also the source of our greatest struggles. It's likely that right now, you can think of one person with whom you have some sort of conflict. Yet, at the very same moment, you can think of someone who has blessed you greatly.

Many authors and teachers have used the analogy of velvet and sandpaper in helping us see the purpose of all people for our personal growth. The velvet relationships are those that make us feel good about ourselves. They make us shine. The sandpaper, however, are rough and abrasive. They are the people who "rub us the wrong way." As self-centered, self-preserving people, we want all the velvet friendships we can get. But we want all the sandpaper people out of our lives—now! While we hate to admit it, the things that bother us the most in others are typically also our own bad habits and qualities. But as God works in our lives, both types of people serve his purposes.

For Teri, J.D. bringing Samantha and Lily home was a sandpaper moment of which she did not want any part. But God had a plan.

The morning after their first night at J.D. and Teri's home, Lily is spinning down the hallway, holding a ballerina doll she found while exploring. While mimicking the pictures of Kathleen—the couple's daughter who died years earlier—that line the hall in various ballet poses, Lily is deep in the midst of a pirouette. She doesn't see Teri until she nearly runs into her. Both are startled.

Lily, looking at Kathleen's pictures, says, "She's so pretty." Teri, still a proud mother, responds, "Yes, she was." Even at her young age, the little girl realizes the sadness on Teri's face. Apologetic, Lily softly reassures, "I'll try not to remind you of her." Teri, feeling the pain being overcome by love, drops to her knees and sweeps Lily into an embrace. "Don't you worry about that, sweetheart," she says. "You just be yourself and everything will be fine."

"As iron sharpens iron, so a friend sharpens a friend" (Proverbs 27:17 NLT). As we read this verse, if we were to ask, "Is the friend here a velvet or a sandpaper relationship?" we wouldn't know, would we? The truth is it could be either one.

If you take a dull knife and a sharper one and begin to rub the blades against each other for the purpose of sharpening, the reality is both are going to be sharpened in the process. Even in mentoring relationships where an older and wiser person is pouring into a younger one, both are blessed by the interaction and learn from each other. Iron sharpens iron—both ways.

Lily is blessed by the generosity of Teri and the newfound sense of belonging, but Teri's heart is now open to a healing love for the first time in years. Iron sharpens iron—both ways.

Maybe today it's time to reevaluate those sandpaper relationships and see the opportunity God may be giving you to grow in a manner your velvet ones may not offer. But, also, now is a good time to think about your velvet friendships and be grateful.

Consider these thoughts about relationships:

People will hurt us, but people will help us.

When we get hurt, we can begin to shut out all relationships. This is never a valid solution.

People will leave us, but people will come into our lives.

We all have an exit door and an entry door in our hearts. While we will never be able to stop anyone who decides to leave us, we must always look for those who are trying to come in and get to know us as well.

People will bless us, while people will burden us.

The closer someone gets to us, the more they may become both a blessing and a burden. We will be as well to those who love us. We must be grateful for those who bless while finding God's purpose for the ones who burden.

Complete these thoughts in your journal:

My top velvet relationships are …

My top sandpaper relationships are …

God, today I see that, in my relationships, you are showing me …

LEAVING LASTING IMPRESSIONS

Lacey and Carlos are walking and talking in the park, continuing to explore their newfound relationship. Carlos begins sharing about the sounds, emotions, and horrors of war that he experienced as a Marine. He realizes he's gripping the rail of a small footbridge tight enough that his knuckles are white. Lacey is staring intently at him. "You okay?" she asks. Carlos hesitates, then decides she deserves an honest response. "Not really." Her concern deepens. "Bad memory?" "Something like that," he says. Lacey softly reassures, "I'm a good listener."

In one of our previous days, we took a look at how to listen to God. As our culture becomes faster, crazier, and more self-focused, the art of listening is quickly being lost. With all the many distractions in our midst, including whatever digital device we are tethered to at the moment, truly listening through human interaction is threatened today in a manner unlike any time in history. Someone can be right in front of us talking, but we might choose instead to stare at a small screen. A person can be sharing with us, and our internal noise just drowns out their words. We're all guilty of this; it's just a matter of how much. And the younger a person is, the greater the temptation to tune out.

A term connected to this epidemic of interaction that has worked its way into our vocabulary over the past decade is "digital footprint." Simply defined, this is the trail we leave online. Techies tell us even when we delete any file or page, though it may disappear from view, it still exists, even when history is "erased." Work and wishes, secrets and shopping, habits and hobbies, all displayed in our digital footprint.

But let's consider another print we leave in life—the kind Carlos and Lacey were making on each other. Human impressions. These stick with people. They can often go unseen, yet they never go away. These impressions occur when we stop and truly listen proactively to someone. We focus. We engage. We pay attention. We actually care. While our culture is flying too fast, we must daily look for opportunities to make human impressions.

Lastly, let's bring in another way to touch people—the way a Christ-follower should. Let's call it the "Jesus handprint." This goes deeper than an impression, because we are attempting to touch someone with Jesus' love. We create something eternal when we touch someone's life in his name. Here are a few ways we can make both a human impression and a Jesus handprint:

- Word of encouragement
- Helping hand
- Listening ear
- Prayer for strength
- Financial help
- Gift of the gospel

The Jesus handprint reveals much about our lives by showing how much we love him and how much we love people.

Depth and devotion, faith and focus, care and commitment are all displayed in our Jesus handprint.

Eventually over years, our digital footprint will be covered up byte by byte. Even human impressions can slowly fade away in memories. But the Jesus handprints we make on people will truly be etched in eternity. In fact, in the end, those will be the only ones that actually count.

> Don't run up debts, except for the huge debt of love you owe each other. When you love others, you complete what the law has been after all along. The law code—don't sleep with another person's spouse, don't take someone's life, don't take what isn't yours, don't always be wanting what you don't have, and any other "don't" you can think of—finally adds up to this: Love other people as well as you do yourself. You can't go wrong when you love others. When you add up everything in the law code, the sum total is love.
> —Romans 13:8–10 MSG

Today you will likely leave a long trail of digital footprints. But be mindful also of the human impressions you have opportunity to make. And, first and foremost, leave Jesus handprints on anyone and everyone you can, showing his love and grace to a world desperately hurting and seeking someone to just listen to their hearts.

⊹

In your journal, list three people you know you will encounter today and a plan of action of what you can do to show Jesus to each one.

FOCUSING
ON THE "FORS"

Since the days Christ walked on the earth, man has attempted to discredit him and argue his divinity. One of the popular trends of ridicule today is to call those who proclaim Christ "narrow-minded" and "intolerant." Those wielding this accusation usually believe there are many ways to God, so the focus is placed on the path *you* choose to God, rather than what *God himself* has said. These folks believe whether you choose Spiritual Path A, B, or C, because you have attempted to "reach God," he should honor such a noble effort and allow access to him. Obviously, to disbelieve the truth of Scripture and that Jesus is who he claimed to be is taking a great risk, yet many are willing.

Pastor Matthew is in his office on the phone with his wife. Suddenly the muzzle of a pistol is inches from his face. Kriminal is holding the gun, wanting his stolen money back that Pretty Boy had turned in to the pastor. Though struck with fear, he works hard to not allow it to translate through his voice to Grace. He tells her, "I have to go," as he hangs up. He looks at Kriminal, who grits out, "My money?" "It's right here. I haven't touched it," Matthew says while reaching down and handing him the bag.

The gang leader taunts, "What do you think Jesus would say about you taking my money?" "I think he knows I didn't want it in the first place," Matthew answers back. "So you believe in Jesus?" "I do," Matthew answers assuredly. Kriminal continues, "And you believe if I pull this trigger, you gonna see him?" "Yes. I believe we all will—sooner or later," the pastor declares, now sensing God's strength. "Well, I'm sure you'll understand me hoping you're wrong," Kriminal states as he heads out the door with the bag.

Kriminal said he hopes the pastor is wrong; he did not admit that he is right in his unbelief. Why would someone word a spiritually charged statement this way? Likely because he doesn't have a belief in anything outside of his own realm of ability or possibility. It is the same as saying, "I have no idea what to be right about, but I just hope you're wrong and I don't ever have to face God."

Over the past several decades in ever-increasing measure, those who oppose Christianity, along with even some inside the faith, have focused far more energy on what Scripture is *against* rather than what it is *for*. As any culture becomes more rebellious at its core, any sort of rule or law will receive a focus of hatred.

Here are just a few encouraging "fors" in our faith:

God sent Jesus to save the world, not to condemn it (see John 3:17).

God's heart is for all his children to receive his gift of salvation (see 1 Timothy 2:3–4).

Jesus wants everyone to be with him wherever he is—fellowship in this life and heaven forever (see John 17:24).

Jesus wants to give everyone a full and meaningful life (see John 10:10).

God wants to give his children good gifts—qualities and blessings that could only come from his hand (see Matthew 7:9–11).

Because God is a loving Father, his Word is filled with promises of blessing that we must keep in the forefront of our hearts, minds, and conversations. In the end, Pastor Matthew is right. Sooner or later, we will all face God, and what we have chosen to believe about Jesus will make all the difference.

Then God gave Christ the highest place and honored his name above all others. So at the name of Jesus everyone will bow down, those in heaven, on earth, and under the earth. And to the glory of God the Father everyone will openly agree, "Jesus Christ is Lord!" —Philippians 2:9–11 CEV

Finish out these sentences in your journal:
Jesus, I believe in you today because …
Father, my favorite "for" that you offer me is …

UNLIMITED INCEPTION

I n a tense, potentially dangerous confrontation with Krimi-nal, Pretty Boy makes a profound and prolific declaration: "We don't have to be who we were."

We would have a difficult time finding a better, simpler explanation of what the good news of the gospel offers us all. There are two ways this statement embodies truth:

We don't have to be who we were … forevermore.

When Jesus comes into our lives, everything changes. Who we once were is gone and a new life is born. The process of transformation starts immediately.

This means that anyone who belongs to Christ has become a new person. The old life is gone; a new life has begun! —2 Corinthians 5:17 NLT

We don't have to be who we were … yesterday.

Each day is a fresh opportunity to let go of the failures of the past, to grow and press on in Christ. As the old saying goes: yesterday is gone and tomorrow never comes. All we have is today.

> But if we confess our sins to God, he can always
> be trusted to forgive us and take our sins away.
> —1 John 1:9 CEV

What an amazing transaction God offers those who are in Christ: we sin, we confess to him and agree we have been disobedient, then he forgives and cleanses us of the wrong, as if it never happened. This does not mean he will remove all consequences of a poor decision, but he takes away the sin from our soul, removing all condemnation, guilt, and shame. The quite amazing fact of this promise is there is no quantity limit. He offers us total forgiveness from the day of salvation to the day of entering heaven.

Is there anything from your "old life" that you have not been able to shake off in your "new life"? A very common issue we all face upon salvation is being able to quickly shed certain vices and habits, while others seem to plague us continually, some for many years. Any sin that continues to create constant temptation likely needs more intense and focused help than you have previously been giving the issue. Here are a few helps for victory given in three Cs:

1: Confession. Many people keep sins a secret, making the battle almost impossible to win, because they are always fighting alone ... and losing. Consider disclosing this problem with a trusted spiritual leader or friend, then praying together about it on a regular basis for a season. Sometimes just getting a problem outside yourself will free you to find victory.

2: *Coalesce.* Coalesce means to take action together; to come together for a common purpose; to join forces. This is a step past disclosure that creates accountability, giving another person permission to help you take action against an issue. Confession places no burden on the other individual besides to listen, care, and pray. Coalesce contains these three elements but adds action.

3: *Counseling.* There are times when all of these steps with a peer or leader do not stop a constant area of sin. Christian counseling can be a powerful tool in the hands of God to unlock truth and shed light on the reasons for some behavior. The days of there being a stigma on those who seek out counseling are over. Many issues plaguing someone for years can be ended in only a few counseling sessions.

As we close today, thank God "you don't have to be who you were" ever again!

Take a moment to write down in your journal any sins from which you were able to see victory soon after accepting Christ.

Next, write down any with which you are currently struggling.

Lastly, thank God for the victories you have experienced through him. Thank him for new life and for forgiveness of all sin. Pray to have victory over the areas you wrote down as you seek to confess, coalesce with a trusted person, or seek counseling.

NO SILENCE
FOR SAINTS

Pretty Boy continues to share his newfound faith with Kriminal, who is growing more agitated with each word. "Shut up about Jesus, P.B. I mean it!" "I can't. And I won't. He loves you."

Peter and John were publicly telling people about Jesus when some priests and Sadducees walked up with the captain of the temple guard. They didn't like all the talk of Christ's resurrection and were growing increasingly disturbed by how the people were responding en masse. Feeling threatened by the groundswell of faith, they grabbed the two disciples and threw them in jail.

The next day, the teachers of the law, led by Annas, the high priest, called for Peter and John to be brought before them. The leaders were particularly concerned about the healing of a lame man for whom the two were responsible. "By what power or what name did you do this?" they asked. Inspired by the Holy Spirit, Peter gave a brief message, but his answer, in short, was "Jesus Christ, whom you crucified." The courage of the two, coupled with a healed man standing as evidence, caused a dilemma. After conferring together, they ordered Peter and John to stop speaking about or in Jesus' name. Their response:

But Peter and John replied, "Which is right in God's eyes: to listen to you, or to him? You be the judges! As for us, we cannot help speaking about what we have seen and heard." —Acts 4:19–20 NIV

The change Christ brings cannot be kept a secret. The gospel is not a private matter to hide, but a public mandate to share.

Because the gospel is of an eternal nature, many people don't want to hear about it, think about it, or deal with it on any level. This negative and adverse reaction can cause many Christians to just "keep it to themselves." After all, why bother people who really don't want to hear it?

What if everyone in your life who knew the gospel—family, friends, pastor, or priest—had chosen to keep it from you ... forever? Your entire life, no one tells you. They decide you don't want to be bothered. They decide it's not worth it. They decide you probably don't want to hear about God anyway.

One of the best motivators for us to not "shut up" about Jesus is reminding ourselves that someone decided to share with us. Someone loved you enough to tell you.

Every few years, statistics are released by a faith-based organization telling us an unchanging truth: the overwhelming majority of people who decide to enter into a relationship with Jesus do so through a relationship with another believer.

Consider these thoughts today:

The message needs a messenger. Every vaccine has to have a delivery method to get to the host. God uses his people as his primary means of delivery of his message of hope, love, and grace.

The message needs a method. There isn't just one way to share the gospel with people. Some people use Bible verses, others share their personal story, while some use a tract or other resource. Churches use music, drama, teaching, benevolence, and countless other ministries to present God's truth. Remember—one message, many methods.

The message needs a measure. An old adage goes: "You may be the only Bible someone reads." Our lives become a standard by which people compare and contrast their own lives and the lives of others. While this can certainly be uncomfortable for us at times, it is a healthy challenge for us to live as a witness for Christ through our attitude and actions as well as our words. People can see if Christianity "works" by watching us.

If you have received Christ's gift of salvation and Lordship, then you are a messenger and a measure, while the method for delivery is open for your own creativity and giftedness. "Speak about what you have heard and seen." Decide you "can't and won't shut up about Jesus."

Complete these sentences in your journal:
Father, the best way I know to share about you and what you have done in my life is by…

Help me to share my faith as soon as possible with …

PROOF POSITIVE

Lacey is beginning to feel hopeless once again as she steps outside onto her rooftop balcony, wrapping herself in a sweater. She stands alone in the rain. Somehow the water feels oddly symbolic as she feels it wash over and quickly cover her entire being. As she reaches her hands into the pockets of the sweater, she feels something inside. Puzzled, she pulls out the small wooden cross Carlos had obviously slipped into her sweater at some point as they shared about life. As Lacey stares at the small icon of hope, her heart feels a glimmer of something she has never experienced before. Then aloud into the pouring night sky she speaks the words, "They say you're God. ... Show me."

God is amazing at responding to this type of prayer. He specializes in them. He doesn't require a pretty, flowery speech to call on his power. "Show me" is all he needs.

> This is God's Message, the God who made earth, made it livable and lasting, known everywhere as God: "Call to me and I will answer you. I'll tell you marvelous and wondrous things that you could never figure out on your own." —Jeremiah 33:3 MSG

There are plenty of people in the world who feel they have life all figured out. They may feel like they don't need a god, or anyone else for that matter. The issue with this mind-set is some problem, coming along when least expected, is going to be bigger than the available resources to fix it. When this happens, the two choices are typically self-destruction or cry for help.

On the other hand, there are plenty of people in the world who feel like they don't have a chance at life and are desperately searching for any answer. Ironically, this person often will not look to God either, because they feel inferior. *Why would God take the time to mess with me at all?* they wonder. So why bother? The problem with this mind-set is that even when things get hopeless, all answers have already been ruled out due to fear and insecurity.

Lacey fits in our latter category. But she has decided to look up ... to God. The only One associated with the cross in her pocket.

God offers everyone in every category the opportunity not only to know him, but also to understand the elusive truths of life that only he can show. Our verse for today makes two distinct promises.

First, if and when we call, he promises to answer. The understanding we must have here is because he is God, he doesn't converse the way we do. You won't hear audible dialogue but rather the conversation of the heart.

Second, God will tell us things we can't know on our own. He will speak to us through:

Our spirit: This is very much like learning a new language, but one you most certainly can discern. As you pray and listen, over time, you will hear his voice.

His Word: The Bible is the inspired Word of God. His promises, commands, principles, and precepts are contained inside. The more we read, study, memorize, and process the contents, the more we can understand and hear his answers for life.

People: Your spiritual leaders and your trusted Christian family, friends, and peers can help you see, hear, and discern God's answers. While you certainly must be careful with this level of trust in others to hear God for you, he most certainly will use relationships to speak to you.

Circumstances: Just like with people, God can orchestrate circumstances in your life to lead you. Oftentimes the invitation is also the calling.

Lacey was finally reaching out for life, not death. She was walking in the right direction for salvation, no longer destruction. God knows what to do with "show me" prayers. But he doesn't stop once we know him. He continues to answer these prayers all throughout our lives to lead us in his ways.

Finish this open-ended sentence on your journal page:
God, I call out to you today for …
Take a moment and write down something the Lord is showing you in your life through his Spirit to yours, his Word, a person, or circumstances.

LEAVING ENEMY TERRITORY

With the meteoric rise of social media and people hiding behind anonymity becoming the new norm, the practice of bullying is at an all-time high. This concept has radically changed how we view enemies. An enemy could be a personal friend with whom you have had a severe conflict or a total stranger who targets your social media page. Random acts of violence occur on the freeway, in shopping malls, and at workplaces. Rage knows no boundaries. No one is exempt from the possibility of an attack, whether it is in cyberspace or in personal space. Revenge, anger, bitterness, jealousy, and violence are all fast and frequent friends to our world today.

Because of this growing epidemic, followers of Christ have the same increased temptations as anyone, but are also offered an amazing opportunity to act radically different than the culture. Today a kind, patient, and gentle person will "stick out" in the world. As bad gets worse, good looks even better.

Bobby turns and spots Andrea. As he approaches, she looks at him, baffled. She musters her courage, swallows some pride, and asks, "You saved my life. Why?" Bobby pauses, then with a slight smile, answers, "Matthew 5:44." Andrea gives back a confused look. "Let me save you the trouble. 'Love your enemies and pray for those who persecute you.'" He reaches into his pocket, takes out his little wooden cross, hands it to her, and with assurance, promises, "I'll be praying for you, Andrea."

Bobby's response rocked Andrea's world and showed the distinct difference Christ can make in a heart. Loving someone who has hurt us is against everything our flesh stands for. In Matthew 5:44, Jesus was letting everyone know God's brand of love is countercultural and unconditional. The only way we could possibly love an enemy and pray for them is to love through God's love, not our own.

A verse in Proverbs that distinguishes evil from good and ally from enemy separates people into two groups: plotters and planners.

> Do not those who plot evil go astray? But those who plan what is good find love and faithfulness.
> —Proverbs 14:22 NIV

A plot is a private agenda with a selfish motive, scheming to hide the truth.

A plan is an intentional public action, providing opportunity for the best to all involved.

God is definitely about planning and Satan is most certainly into plotting. The goal would be the more mature we become in Christ, the less we plot and the more we plan.

Here are a couple of examples of the difference:

A plotter hides important details of a business dealing, while a planner lays everything on the table and answers all questions truthfully.

A plotter tries to quietly criticize the pastor's new plan for the Sunday schedule to drum up opposition, while the planner makes an appointment with the pastor to hear out the details, then shares any remaining concerns firsthand.

Andrea was openly plotting against Bobby for her own gain and agenda. Bobby was risking everything, trusting God had a much bigger plan for him than he could see at the time.

We are tempted daily to plot, although God always offers the plan. You've probably heard the saying, "Failing to plan is planning to fail." Consider these three points:

1: A solid plan keeps you away from the temptation to plot.

2: A solid plan can keep you from falling victim to someone else's plot. (Don't let someone else have a better plot than your plan.)

3: A solid plan is provided daily by God himself.

The good news is planners are just redeemed plotters.

Plan to love your enemies and pray for them; don't plot evil to repay. Today, look for love and faithfulness in others, while others find love and faithfulness in you.

In your journal, complete these three sentences:
Father, I confess I consider this person (or persons) my enemy …
Father, I pray for my enemies now by saying …
Father, I plan on showing love and faithfulness to …

ARE YOU MISSING SOMETHING?

D r. Farell had just left Joe's room after calling the time of death. As he steps from the elevator, the stairwell door flies open. Elena rushes out, looking like she just ran all the way. "Doctor! There's something you need to see … Joe Philips." The doctor looks puzzled, then asks, "The one whose certificate I just signed?" Elena nods a hesitant, yet surprised yes. Farell questions, "Why? Did I miss something?" The nurse responds, "You could say that."

The "something" that mankind all too often misses is God. When he is brought into any situation, "something" happens. From the mundane to the miraculous, God's intervention changes people and the outcome.

Jesus' good friends Mary and Martha had a brother named Lazarus. He had become very ill, so the sisters sent word to see if Jesus could come. Upon his arrival, Lazarus had already been dead for four days. The sisters, along with a large group of mourners, met Jesus at the tomb. Many began confessing that had he gotten there sooner, he could have saved Lazarus. While this certainly showed great faith from the people, they were placing a limitation on Christ by thinking death was an irreversible condition for him. As they removed the stone from the tomb …

Jesus looked up and said, "Father, I thank You for hearing Me. I know You always hear Me. But I have said this for the people standing here, so they may believe You have sent Me." When He had said this, He called with a loud voice, "Lazarus, come out!" The man who had been dead came out. His hands and feet were tied in grave clothes. A white cloth was tied around his face. Jesus said to the people, "Take off the grave clothes and let him go!" —John 11:41–44 NLV

When Jesus told the people to roll the stone away from Lazarus' tomb, I wonder if anyone said, "Why? Did we miss something?" just as Dr. Farell had questioned.

Once again, we see the "something" missed was God's limitless power to change circumstances. Dr. Farell thought he and the staff had done everything possible to save Joe. The family and friends gathered at Lazarus' home knew had Jesus only come sooner, he might have been able to heal him. Can you imagine standing at that tomb and seeing Lazarus walk out in his mummy outfit? That would have been "something!"

The practical point for today is this: even as Christians, we too easily factor God out of our everyday lives. We miss him and the "something" he can add to so many situations throughout our day.

Every single day, God wants to intervene in your life to work… in you.

God wants full access to your heart to rid you of sin and death—the things that keep you from experiencing the full life he has to offer. He wants you to submit your will to him to sweep out every room, clean out every closet, and haul off any junk you have accumulated and are hanging on to that only causes hurt and pain.

Every single day, God wants to intervene in your life to work… on you.

He wants to give you the qualities of his Son, Jesus. God wants to give you the fruit of the Spirit from Galatians 5: love, joy, peace, patience, kindness, gentleness, faithfulness, goodness, and self-control. Jesus wants people to see him "on you" when they look at your life.

Every single day, God wants to intervene in your life to work… through you.

Once God has made headway by working in you and on you, then he can start to work through you. He can use you to do his work, minister to others, and make a difference in the world. Who doesn't want to change the world? And who better to work with than God himself?

Is it time to hear Jesus say this about you? "Take the grave clothes off and let him/her go!"

In your journal, write down a situation in your life right now where God is working *in you*.

Then, write down a situation where he is working *on you*.

And lastly, write down a situation where he is working *through you*.

REMOVING ROADBLOCKS

After Dr. Farell and nurse Elena rush back into Joe's room to find him awake and alert, the stoic and self-reliant MD is struggling with an explanation for what he has just witnessed. Finally, Joe says, "Doc, the man whose death certificate you signed is sitting here talking to you ... and you don't believe in miracles? I'm just saying ... you might wanna reconsider." Joe reaches for the small wooden cross on his nightstand and offers it to Farell with humility and gentleness, as well as a symbol of explanation for what has taken place. The doctor just stares at Joe's offering for a moment and then turns on his heels and walks out.

The sad truth is some people in this world just don't want salvation—from anything, anywhere, at any time. Or if they do, they want it completely on their terms—not God's. The word *pride* has an *I* right in the middle of its spelling for a reason. While this can be hard to accept, we must remember we are only responsible for communication of the gospel through word and actions; we are not held accountable for anyone's actual salvation. God gives every person free will to choose his or her own way. We must respectfully do the same.

One day a wealthy young ruler walked up to Jesus and asked

how he could inherit eternal life. Jesus responded by referring to the Ten Commandments. Here is the rest of that encounter:

> "All these I have kept since I was a boy," he said. When Jesus heard this, he said to him, "You still lack one thing. Sell everything you have and give to the poor, and you will have treasure in heaven. Then come, follow me." When he heard this, he became very sad, because he was very wealthy. Jesus looked at him and said, "How hard it is for the rich to enter the kingdom of God!" —Luke 18:21–24 NIV

Jesus wasn't after this man's money at all, but his heart. He knew the giant roadblock that his possessions and power had built between the man and God. Essentially, he told him how to clear the path to his soul and find salvation.

Dr. Farell had full trust and reliance on one person—himself. Then his gifts and skills for healing only complicated his magnification of himself. God knew he had to be shown unmistakable evidence that he had been wrong as a doctor. Something or Someone was bigger than his intellect and prowess as a physician.

After the ruler turned on his heels and walked away from Jesus ...

> Those who heard this asked, "Who then can be saved?" Jesus replied, "What is impossible with man is possible with God." —Luke 18:26–27 NIV

Everyone's story of salvation is unique. While the end result is the same, the journey is always different. Here are a few suggestions of ways to reach out to people with the gospel:

Invite to church or small group.
Invite regularly to dinner, coffee, or other social interaction.
Befriend, listen, care, and communicate.
Engage in a common activity of interest.
Provide help or acts of service.
Show interest and support of their career or activities.

Find an area of service close to the person's heart and invite to engage.

Here are three areas of focus to remove spiritual roadblocks for people:

1: Pray. There is no greater work to be offered on anyone's behalf than prayer. Intercede for the person and against the roadblocks.

2: Love. Unconditional and sacrificial love is the greatest tool in the hand of God for building someone's eternity with him.

3: Tell. Any opportunity to connect the person to a spiritual moment through words should be taken with respect, care, and honor—to the person and to God.

Take a moment to think back to your own salvation. In your journal, write down your biggest roadblock to God that had to be cleared for you to see him.

Next, write down the names of three people you want to see come to Christ. Beside each name, write down what you feel his or her roadblock might be.

Close by praying for each person and for God to use you to reach them.

THE VERY VISIBLE VERSE

Andrea is sitting alone on a table in the hospital. She's shaken up, but it's her soul that is the most turned upside down. She's deep in thought, staring at her phone. But this time, it's not a text or a social media update she's reading. She has pulled up a Bible verse. We're not certain, but it might be the only one she knows. But if so, it's a good one. The classic—John 3:16 (NKJV):

> For God so loved the world that He gave His only begotten Son, that whoever believes in Him should not perish but have eternal life.

This verse is the most widely known and memorized Bible verse in history. We've seen it emblazoned in a multitude of public places in many forms. What is it about this one verse that grabs the hearts of humans, intrigues us, and causes us to display or quote it?

One reason is likely because John did an amazing and anointed job of getting the gospel message into a single verse. Let's take it apart and look a bit deeper …

For God...

He saw the problem created by sin and was proactive to redeem us. God does the work of salvation. Never should anyone say, "I found God!" God has never been lost; He finds us. He saves us. We simply need to be grateful and declare, "God found me!"

... so loved ...

His great love was the driving force empowering the mission of Jesus. Isn't it awesome that God's motivation was not anger or anything *against* us, but fully and completely *for* us?

... the world ...

Throughout history; through all generations; in every nation, tribe, and language; God came first to the Jewish people, then to the Gentile. The worship word *hallelujah* is the same in every language and every dialect, to reflect the universal offer he makes to all.

... that he gave ...

God gave everything needed and required by his own standards for us to be saved. We can do nothing on our own. We cannot make it to God on our own. He gave so we can be saved. His gift made redemption possible.

... His only begotten Son ...

There is only one place in Scripture where God asks a man to sacrifice his son. But as Genesis 22 unfolds, we see as Abraham raises the knife to kill his son, Isaac, God stops him and provides a ram caught in a bush for the substitution and sacrifice. God was only testing Abraham. But when God placed his Son on the cross, he went through with the sacrifice. Jesus was the Lamb who was slain for the sins of the world.

... that whoever believes in him ...

Everyone. Anyone. Regardless of age, gender, race, or any other distinction we may make, God shows no favoritism. This truth alone eliminates racism or classism as a part of a believer's worldview. Heaven will have one classification— those who believe and are saved.

... should not perish ...

Sin and death are no longer an eternal threat. Salvation has come and rescue is here. As Isaiah 61:1 tells us, "He has sent me to bind up the brokenhearted, to proclaim freedom for the captives and release from darkness for the prisoners" (NIV).

... but have eternal life.

God has opened his home to us with an opportunity for eternity. Jesus said in John 14:2, "My Father's house has many rooms; if that were not so, would I have told you that I am going there to prepare a place for you?" (NIV)

Yes, if Andrea was going to pull up just one Bible verse to consider God and his plan for her life, John 3:16 is certainly one of the best to find.

Write your name in the blanks below and then read this personalized version of the verse.

For God so loved _____that He gave His only begotten Son, that [because] _____believes in Him, [he/she] shall not perish, but have eternal life.

In your journal, write out a thank-you note to God for your personal salvation and the room he has prepared for you in his house forever.

CONCENTRIC COMMUNITY

J.D.'s wheelchair rolls into the room as Teri is pushing from behind. It's a joyous moment for everyone—Joe, Samantha, Lily, Teri, and J.D.—like a brand-new family reunion. Lily is beside herself because she has seen God answer every prayer she has prayed. But she's not the only one to take notice.

Grinning ear to ear, Lily says, "See mommy? God really does love us!" Samantha, feeling a sense of peace and real joy she hasn't felt in a very long time, answers her, "Yes, he does, baby. He really does."

Mary Magdalene met Jesus in a very unusual way too. To be blunt, she was demon-possessed; with not just one, but seven spirits. Her life was literally a living hell—until she crossed paths with the Christ.

Jesus freed Mary from her bondage and turmoil. To say she was grateful for her healing would be an understatement. She stayed near to Jesus. When his disciples ran away from the cross, she was there with Jesus' mother. She was the first one at the tomb, the first one to encounter the risen Christ.

She turned to leave and saw someone standing there. It was Jesus, but she didn't recognize him. "Dear woman, why are you crying?" Jesus asked her. "Who are you looking for?" She thought he was the gardener. "Sir," she said, "if you have taken him away, tell me where you have put him, and I will go and get him." "Mary!" Jesus said. She turned to him and cried out, "Rabboni!" (which is Hebrew for "Teacher"). "Don't cling to me," Jesus said, "for I haven't yet ascended to the Father. But go find my brothers and tell them, 'I am ascending to my Father and your Father, to my God and your God.'" Mary Magdalene found the disciples and told them, "I have seen the Lord!" Then she gave them his message. —John 20:14–18 NLT

Based on Samantha's response to Lily, we can be confident she could join Mary Magdalene's declaration of "I have seen the Lord!" We can also be confident she will be able to "give his message" by telling others what she has seen and heard.

Everyone knows the old saying: "Blood is thicker than water," meaning family will stick together over friends; but there is a bond created among believers that goes beyond family or friends—thicker than blood or water. The reason so many of the characters in the film *Do You Believe?* became close so quickly and overcame any differences or barriers is the bond the blood of Christ creates. Realizing you have a connection with another person in your walk with Jesus lays a foundation for a relationship unlike any other. Many believers who share in their spiritual journeys become far closer than family and friends.

To experience the sense of community that Joe, Samantha, Lily, Teri, and J.D. did, as well as what Mary Magdalene had with Jesus and his disciples, let's consider the three Es of biblical community:

Engage. The only way we are going to experience real community and fellowship is to proactively seek it out. We have to decide to trade isolation for interaction, seclusion for serving one another. Jesus came to save the world, but he lived life fully engaged with his band of disciples.

Exchange. In this digital age of cyber segregation, face-to-face, knee-to-knee interaction is a dying art, yet it is still an innate need in us all. From the tribal fires to the campfire to the dinner table, sitting down and sharing life has always been a crucial part of how God comforts us, coerces us, and even convicts us.

Execute. What good is faith if it's not lived out and witnessed? Engaging with other believers and exchanging life's blessings and burdens has to have an appropriate end. As a Christ-follower, that means only one thing—executing his work into the world.

Blood may be thicker than water, but Christ's blood in us draws us to closeness unlike any other relationship available this side of heaven.

In your journal, list at least three people with whom you experience biblical community and write down how they encourage your faith. Then the next time you have opportunity, let them know.

LORD OF "THE RINGS"

Today is focused on marriages, but if you are single, please read on to apply the principles to your key relationships. After all, truth is truth.

Bobby steps into the hospital chapel. The room is small, but inviting. He looks at the cross for a moment and then is surprised to find Elena, his wife, sitting at the altar. He softly asks, "Hey there. What are you doing in here?" She answers, "Praying." Trying not to sound too surprised, Bobby simply utters, "Oh?" "Well, not praying, exactly," she explains. "More like apologizing," she continues as tears begin to well up. "Tonight, I saw a miracle. A real-life, *en carne viva* miracle, and it made me realize how I've been acting—like the God who did that somehow wouldn't be there for us. I felt ashamed and then I realized: I don't wanna live like this anymore. I wanna give Jesus my whole life—all of it. No more holding back." Bobby, amazed at the answered prayers, wraps his arms around Elena. "I'm the one who should be apologizing," he says. "I've been so busy sharing my faith with everyone else. I somehow lost sight of you ... forgive me?" "Sure," she softly responds. Bobby then asks, "Now will you pray with me?" "Gladly," she answers.

Bobby and Elena's moment in the chapel—their best moment in quite a long time— shows us some key elements of a successful marriage.

*1: **Mutual dependence on God.*** Both were placing God before themselves and their spouse. God is the head of the marriage, so they can function and think correctly when everything is properly lined up. Submitting to God together brings a peace and joy to the common foundation he lays in a marriage.

*2: **Mutual submission to one another.*** Marriage is not a battle for rights, but a blessing of righteousness. When each spouse places the other first, then forgiveness, growth, joy, peace, and an ever-increasing love can become a reality and not just a romantic notion.

> In the original creation, God made male and female to be together. Because of this, a man leaves father and mother, and in marriage he becomes one flesh with a woman—no longer two individuals, but forming a new unity. Because God created this organic union of the two sexes, no one should desecrate his art by cutting them apart. —Mark 10:6–9 MSG

The biblical concept of marriage truly is a miraculous covenant. God takes two people and, while maintaining their separate identities, forms a new union of the two. The Message Bible paints a beautiful word picture by calling marriage "his art."

A great way to depict this level of bonding between a man and a woman can be illustrated by duct tape. If you take a roll of gray duct tape, measure out two equal strips, cut them from the roll, then carefully line up all four edges to stick them together, you have a permanent bonding. There is no way to get those two strips of duct tape apart without completely destroying both original pieces. The bonding of the two strips of tape creates a virtually indestructible union. The NIV Bible conveys the Mark 10:9 verse by saying, "Therefore what God has joined together, let no one separate." When you see two pieces of duct tape matched and stuck perfectly together, this verse has a whole new meaning, because regardless of someone's strength, the two can't be pulled apart again.

A major goal of God's plan for marriage is to make us into his image. Few things in this world can change us into the image of Christ faster than the person we love the most encouraging and inspiring us to be like Jesus.

One of the best marriage steps you can take that statistically proves to hold marriages together is praying, as Bobby asked Elena to do. Praying regularly about life can keep you both focused and faithful to God and each other.

In your journal, rate your marriage on a scale from 1 to 10 for:
  Mutual dependence on God _____
  Mutual submission to each other _____
  Write down one action step you can take this week to be more obedient to God in your marriage. Write down your most pressing prayer request for your marriage, and then pray.
  If you are single, write down one action step you can take toward your relationship with God and in your friendships. Write down your most pressing prayer request for yourself, and then pray.

THE FABRIC
OF FAMILY AND FAITH

The people we love are going to make good choices that bless us and bad choices that hurt us. This is a fact of life. And no matter how much we would like to avoid and control the painful times, they come—often when we least expect them.

One of the most difficult circumstances we deal with is when a loved one chooses to turn his or her back on God. We can talk, pray, hope, and agonize over someone's soul, only to watch the person grow more hardened to the gospel. While this can feel quite personal after a while, it isn't; what he or she does with Jesus is up to that person. As they say: all we can do is all we can do. Keep praying and showing love.

Dr. Farell enters the hospital room where Andrea is waiting. She continues to stare at the Bible verse on her phone screen. He asks, "Are you okay?" Andrea replies, "Actually, no. I'm not." Farell, flipping on his doctor switch, fires back, "What is it? Are you hurt?" as he approaches to examine her. But Andrea raises her hand, signaling that is not what she needs, and then continues, "What kind of person would risk his life for someone who just finished ruining him?" Dr. Farell, obviously not wanting to go "there," states in a frustrated tone,

"Can we please just go?" Andrea's heart won't let her let go, as she says firmly, "No. ... I think I've been wrong, Thomas. And I think you have too." He snaps, "Honestly, Andrea. What is wrong with you?"

> Those who declare publicly that they belong to me, I will do the same for them before my Father in heaven. But those who reject me publicly, I will reject before my Father in heaven. Do not think that I have come to bring peace to the world. No, I did not come to bring peace, but a sword. I came to set sons against their fathers, daughters against their mothers, daughters-in-law against their mothers-in-law; your worst enemies will be the members of your own family. Those who love their father or mother more than me are not fit to be my disciples; those who love their son or daughter more than me are not fit to be my disciples. Those who do not take up their cross and follow in my steps are not fit to be my disciples. —Matthew 10:32–38 GNT

As he did in much of his teaching, Jesus draws a "line in the sand" in regard to following him. However, he is not advocating or condoning turning your back on your family; in fact, Jesus' influence on our lives should only increase our capacity to love and serve. He is simply stating we should place him first and love him above all our relationships. This keeps relational priorities in proper order.

There will be times, though, that the cross becomes a point of separation, even in families. Many want nothing to do with Jesus, so therefore want nothing to do with a family member who follows him. Conflicting lifestyles can make it very difficult to live in peace. While we should always focus on being the best witness possible, there are times when healthy boundaries must be put into place. It sounds like Andrea was about to put such a boundary between her and Dr. Farell.

We can see clearly, even in such a brief encounter as Andrea and the doctor had, when Jesus begins to draw someone, the division for some becomes insurmountable. If this has happened to you because of your faith, first, be encouraged that your belief is showing to such a level. But then, continue to show love, grace, and care to express the proof of Christ in your life. Maybe some day, he or she will be ready and you can then be the connection to Jesus.

In your journal, make a list of your family members who need to know Jesus or return to their faith in him. Use the list to regularly pray for them and be creative about the ways you can express Christ's love, even if any of the relationships are strained due to differences in faith.

THE FAITH FACTOR

Pastor Matthew is reflecting on all that has happened in such a short time since he accepted the challenge from Malachi. He shares, "I'm not sure any of us ever gets to see the whole picture. God's eye view, so to speak. It's like we're little children, sitting on the floor, gazing up at the backside of a tapestry that's being woven. To our eyes, it sometimes looks ugly; the colors are a jumble and none of it makes much sense. But one day, we'll no longer be sitting on the floor. We'll come around to the other side, and the genius of God's handiwork will become clear. At the center of it all, we'll see the cross."

When God told ...

... Noah to build an ark because he was going to flood the earth, he had no idea when—or if—it would begin to rain.

... Abram to gather his family and go to a place he would be shown, he had no idea where he was going or what might happen there.

... Joseph the meanings of Pharaoh's dreams, he had no idea if he would be executed or thrown back into prison.

... Moses to demand Pharaoh let his people go, he had no idea if he would be executed on the spot.

… Joshua to defeat Jericho, he had no idea if the trumpets, marching, and shouting strategy would work.

Of course, we could go on and list these same statements about many. It can become tempting to make the people we read about in Scripture into biblical superheroes, but we must remind ourselves that they were just as human as us. They had doubt, fear, and questions, the same as we would. Let us make the connection that the same God who spoke to these folks and orchestrated their outcomes is also taking care of us today. He is the same God!

When we take all we know about how God moved in the lives of his people, coupled with our own experience as he works in our lives, why don't we have a much easier time showing great faith? Why is it so difficult to believe God for our future when we have continually seen him move in our past?

What is faith? It is the confident assurance that something we want is going to happen. It is the certainty that what we hope for is waiting for us, even though we cannot see it up ahead. —Hebrews 11:1 TLB

Every one of the people listed earlier from the Bible dealt with fear on some level when God spoke. Fear is a natural human response to the unknown. But it is also the opposite of faith—the enemy of faith. When we fear, we convince ourselves that the worst might happen. When we express faith, we tell ourselves that the best will happen.

Denial is the opposite of hope. Denial is the enemy of hope. When we deny something is true or possible, we refuse to see truth. When we hope, we want something to be true or possible and we long for it to be true.

Consider these statements about faith, fear, denial, and hope:

Fear causes us to believe bad things, which are *not* real, do exist.

Faith causes us to believe things we cannot yet see truly *do* exist.

Denial causes us to believe real things do *not* exist.

Hope causes us to believe there is a reality to come that is *better* than our current circumstance.

The tapestry Pastor Matthew was talking about—God's gifts of faith and hope, presented through the cross—remind us daily to believe God is indeed weaving us into his handiwork, even when we can't see it.

In your journal, write down a situation where you believe God spoke to you about something you were praying about.

Write down how you felt *before* you knew what God would do or how he would answer.

Next, write down what you knew about the situation *after* God answered or the situation came about.

Lastly, list the steps you can take today to choose faith and hope, denying your fears even an opportunity to exist.

EMBRACE YOUR PLACE

Yesterday, we read Pastor Matthew's analogy of the tapestry of life God is weaving here. One day we'll be brought around to see God's view and it will all make sense because of the cross. Today, we continue his thoughts …

"But in that immense tapestry, we'll also see the single, unique thread—the only one of its kind and color—that our own life has added to the piece; the one thread, without which the whole thing would somehow be incomplete. Personally, I can't wait to see God's masterpiece."

To truly embrace our place in this grand design, we must consider our personal worldview. What each of us believes about the origin of life is crucial to our self-image and identity. Allow me to explain: a person who believes we morphed from monkeys or from a batch of primordial ooze is going to struggle with believing life has much purpose and meaning.

The truth is we are no cosmic collision. We are designed and made by a loving Father who has a plan for each of us. Believing you were created out of a deep love—to both love and be loved—gives purpose, hope, and meaning to life.

Which view actually takes more faith to believe: the world randomly happened, or someone formed all we see with a purpose in mind?

You made all the delicate inner parts of my body and knit them together in my mother's womb. Thank you for making me so wonderfully complex! It is amazing to think about. Your workmanship is marvelous—and how well I know it. You were there while I was being formed in utter seclusion! You saw me before I was born and scheduled each day of my life before I began to breathe. Every day was recorded in your book! —Psalm 139:13–16 TLB

Do you see how someone who feels as the psalmist does has a healthy and balanced sense of purpose and meaning?

Let's review:

God himself formed you in your mother.

Because he formed you, he gave you life. Because he gave you life, he deeply loves you. Because he deeply loves you, he wants a relationship with you. Because he wants a relationship with you, he solved the problem of sin. Because he solved the problem of sin, your life can now be all he intended for it to be when he formed you in your mother!

The Christian worldview believes we are not converts to a religion, but rather friends in a relationship. Therefore, God is intimately involved in the details of our lives and has a plan for each day, as verse 16 states.

Here are three Ws to consider for practical living from this perspective:

1: Walk. Every morning, the best move for us is to put our hand in Jesus' hand and walk with him. No matter who else does or doesn't. This won't be the easiest way, but it will always be the best way.

2: Work. This occurs on two levels. The work we must do to take care of our lives and the work God has called us to. These two areas constantly overlap as we seek to be Christ's ambassadors to the world everywhere we go. Our faith turned into action in the workplace, home, and the world is always important to the kingdom of God.

3: Worship. Recognizing God in all areas of our lives, turning to him, loving him, whether it's a three-second "thank you" under our breath or an hour on-your-face prayer time, is acknowledging his authority in all things. Worship is giving him full reign in our lives and his holy place there.

Our walk with Jesus impacts and empowers our work, bringing worship. Our work creates a dependence on our walk, creating worship. Our worship both flows from and fuels the walk and the work.

Following this simple plan can daily assure us that we are no accident, but an amazing design that God is uniquely using in the world to make a true difference—as Matthew said, creating his masterpiece!

Complete these thoughts in your journal:
God, today in my walk, show me …
God, today in my work, help me …
God, today in my worship, may I …

ONE THING
I KNOW

I n John 9, the story of a blind man healed by Jesus is the focus of the entire chapter. He was walking with people around him and approached this man, whom people evidently knew was born blind. As was the belief of the day, the people felt sin of the man or his parents was to blame for his condition. Jesus made it clear that neither was true, but then he took the focus off the man's problem and put it on his own presence.

Then Jesus did a very curious thing—he bent down, spat in some dirt, took the muddy substance, and placed it on the man's eyes. He then told him to go wash in the Pool of Siloam. The man obeyed, and his eyes were healed!

Now—consider the strangeness that ensued among the people and how no one seemed to recognize a man born blind suddenly and miraculously had his sight.

The people started asking if he was the same man, as if Jesus had played some game of switcheroo. But the man was insistent, telling the story of what Jesus did for him. As the man was questioned further and further, an amazing transformation started to occur in him.

The people decided to take the healed man to the Pharisees, the religious leaders. The day also just happened to be the

Sabbath. When they heard the story, their focus was on a religious law being broken—Jesus had "worked" on the holy day. The Pharisees decided this fully discredited him as a healer. Next, they sent for the man's parents to confirm the story. The parents, afraid for their reputation, essentially "pleaded the fifth" by telling them to ask their son.

The leaders and the people then demanded that the man tell the truth. But he'd finally had enough! In John 9:25, the man brought some practical truth to the insanity when he stated: "One thing I do know. I was blind but now I see!" (NIV)

As he went on to defend Jesus, the Pharisees declared the man a born sinner, announced that they were offended, and threw him out. Jesus found out what had happened and found the man.

> He said, "Do you believe in the Son of Man?" "Who is he, sir?" the man asked. "Tell me so that I may believe in him." Jesus said, "You have now seen him; in fact, he is the one speaking with you." Then the man said, "Lord, I believe," and he worshiped him.
> —John 9:35–38 NIV

Try to imagine being born blind, meeting a man who gives you 20/20 vision, then suddenly being thrust into a religious debate on healing. Might you be in a state of shock too? The man came to the conclusion that he was not only healed, but the healer was the Messiah.

What about your own story? Were you in any sort of difficult physical, emotional, or mental state when Jesus found you? There are times those challenges are what humble us to see God's hand. One thing is true of us all, though—we were spiritually blind in desperate need of our eyes being opened to God. Jesus comes and takes the blindness away, we see him for who he is, and we receive his offer of forgiveness and salvation.

Kriminal is lying in a hospital bed, handcuffed to the metal handrail. In his right hand, he clutches the small cross Pretty Boy got from the church service. Ironically, the cross is now bloodstained. His heart is reeling from all that has happened and what he is now feeling inside.

A detective walks in and asks, "You the one who calls himself Kriminal?"

Pausing, receiving, he answers, "I was ..."

No matter our background, how good or bad we perceived ourselves to be, at the point of faith being birthed in our hearts, we all share the same declaration as the blind man, "*One thing I do know. I was blind but now I see!*" and "*Lord, I believe.*" And then we worship ... forever.

Complete these thoughts in your journal:

Father, some ways I was blind before you saved me were ...

A "blind spot" where I still struggle today and need your healing is ...

Father, thank you that though I was blind, now I can see that ...

AT THE FOOT
OF THE CROSS

When we survey the great, epic battlegrounds through-out history, we never suspect a garden as a likely location. But in two very key places in Scripture, a garden did indeed become a battlefield. Heaven and hell were clashing for the soul of man.

The first battle took place in the garden of Eden.

"You will not surely die," the serpent said to the woman. . . . When the woman saw that the fruit of the tree was good for food and pleasing to the eye, and also desirable for gaining wisdom, she took some and ate it. She also gave some to her husband, who was with her, and he ate it. Then the eyes of both of them were opened. —Genesis 3:4–7 NIV

In mankind's first battle with the enemy, we lost—not because we didn't fight hard enough, but by simply not even lifting a finger. Through the centuries, this battle has raged.

The second battle took place in the garden of Gethsemane.

Jesus said to his disciples, "Sit here while I pray." …
Going a little farther, he fell to the ground and prayed

that if possible the hour might pass from him. "Abba, Father," he said, "everything is possible for you. Take this cup from me. Yet not what I will, but what you will." —Mark 14:32–36 NIV

This battle explains the deep struggle we see and hear in Jesus. From this garden, we take the rest of the story …

After Pilate released Barabbas to his freedom, as the crowd demanded the crucifixion of Christ, they beat him with a cat-of-nine-tails until he was nearly dead. Then the governor's soldiers gathered an entire company around Jesus, stripped him of his robe, fashioned a crown of thorns to place on his head in mockery, and then began their insults. They spit on him and struck him repeatedly on the head with a staff. They then reclothed him, but the material sticking to his open wounds would have been excruciating.

As they led him out to be crucified, seeing that he was in horrendous physical condition, the soldiers grabbed a man named Simon and forced him to carry Jesus' cross. As they came to Golgotha, the place for crucifixions outside of town, it was there they nailed his wrists and feet to the cross, raised it up, and plunged the end into the hole made ready there. Jesus, now beaten, bloody, wracked with pain, and gasping for each breath, took every sin of every person ever in existence upon himself.

From noon until three in the afternoon, the skies now growing dark, he hung there. At three o'clock, he cried out loudly, "My God, my God, why have you forsaken me?" The payment of all sin was coming due at that moment on the person of Jesus.

He cried out once more and then he gave up his spirit. Jesus' life was not taken, no one killed him; he gave up his life. *Paid* was stamped across sin—for good.

As the earth began to respond to the Creator's death by quaking, the centurions who had been standing at the foot of the cross became terrified. One of them cried out, "Surely this man was the Son of God!"

Jesus gained back all that was taken away in the first garden. The Second Adam redeemed the loss of the first Adam.

As we look at the cross, let us come away knowing that we can die to the first Adam and be raised anew in the Second Adam, facing our seemingly endless battles, yet again knowing we can win, only because Jesus has made it possible for us to also confess, "Abba, Father, everything is possible for you."

Malachi is carrying his cross, preaching the Word of God in the same way and with the same fervor as when we first saw him in the glow of Pastor Matthew's headlights. He stops a passerby and asks, "Tell me. Do you believe in the cross of Christ?"

In your final day of journaling here, complete these sentences:

During the past forty days, for me, the cross has come to mean …

Lord Jesus, thank you that the cross has given me …

Heavenly Father, I believe …

TELL YOUR STORY

Congratulations on completing the past forty days! All of us involved with this project pray you now not only believe, but your faith has grown in great measure these past few weeks.

We want to encourage you to continue your new habit of spending time with God daily—reading his Word, praying, listening, applying, and growing in your faith.

May you now have an incredible answer when someone asks you the question, "Do you believe?" And may you ask those you encounter throughout life Malachi's eternal question: "Do you believe in the cross of Christ?"

Tell your story of how you became a part of God's kingdom! Believe!

ABOUT THE AUTHOR

 **ROBERT NOLAND** began his writing career as a songwriter in 1983, then spent the next 10 years as a touring musician and producer, penning lyrics for artists such as Glen Campbell, Babbie Mason, and Gabriel. He wrote his first series of Bible studies in 1988 and in 1991 wrote his first Christian devotional book for a para-church ministry. Noland has since authored over 50 titles spanning across children, youth, and adult audiences. In 1996, he wrote a Christian follow-up booklet entitled *LifeChange*, which to date has sold over one million copies. In 2011, Noland released his first book titled *The Knight's Code* and in 2012 released *3SG*, a Men's Small Group Manual. He blogs regularly at *theknightscode.com*. Since 2011, Noland has been a free-lance writer and author for faith-based organizations, ministries, and Christian publishers. A book co-authored with Randy Frazee, entitled *Think, Act, Believe Like Jesus*, released in December 2014. Regardless of the target audience or mode of delivery via paper or digital, Robert writes what he calls, "practical application of Biblical truth." He lives in Franklin, Tennessee, with his wife of 30 years and has two adult sons. Find him at www.robertnoland.com.